T0197195

FUNDAMENTALS OF WELL-BEING

Four Qualities You Can't Live Without

Patricia Gailey, Ph.D.

BALBOA.PRESS
A DIVISION OF HAY HOUSE

Balboa Press books may be ordered through booksellers or by contacting:

Balboa Press
A Division of Hay House
1663 Liberty Drive
Bloomington, IN 47403
www.balboapress.com
844-682-1282

ISBN: 979-8-7652-3538-6 (sc)
ISBN: 979-8-7652-3539-3 (e)

Balboa Press rev. date: 11/11/2022

For my son

CONTENTS

AUTHOR'S NOTE

My premise in writing this book is that our decisions shape our lives, including our length of life and the quality of our experiences from beginning to end. However, I am acutely aware that many people, particularly Black, Indigenous, and other people of color, have died untimely deaths not because of their own decisions, but because of the unhealthy and unfair decisions of others. My hope is that by raising awareness of how our decisions impact others as well as ourselves there might be fewer tragic and unnecessary events as well as improvement in the quality of life for everyone.

I have no doubt that any truths I have discovered in writing this book are already known to many people. I suspect they are deeply embedded in many Indigenous and other non-European-descent cultural practices. My intention in pursuing this knowledge is to cipher what is true about sustaining life from Western cultural perspectives so that we of European descent can better understand some of what so many others have learned from their ancestors, but without the damaging effect of appropriating of another's cultural knowledge.

In order to claim our own knowledge of how to live in a way that supports ourselves and others we must draw from our own knowledge base. Because science has been given a seat of priority in Western culture, it makes sense to see what science says about how our decisions impact our experience of satisfaction and sustainability. From this knowledge base we can perhaps come into an authentic ownership of some universal truths that others have held across many centuries.

ACKNOWLEDGMENTS

Many thanks to Donna Eder, Margaret Farmer, Joanna Juswik, and Tanya Kell for their valuable feedback.

ILLUSTRATIONS

INTRODUCTION

This book is seeded by a desire to share what I have learned about transforming a long-term trajectory of frustration and unhappiness to an ongoing experience of empowerment. The truth is, every decision we make moves us a step closer to either dying or living. I have made many decisions—thoughtful decisions—that supported my living, and, conversely, many others that moved me toward dying. As an occupational therapist and educator, I have witnessed others also making thoughtful decisions that were well-intended yet ultimately harmful. I wanted to discover why this was and how I and others might make decisions that support living and thriving above all else. This book is about what I have discovered.

Ten years ago I was introduced to Fritjof Capra's book entitled *The Web of Life* and the concept of deep ecology. Deep ecology investigates the interdependent relations of humans with one another as we participate in many communities of various levels of complexity, and with our planetary home. Whereas the term ecology, as commonly understood, considers our impact on our environment, deep ecology probes how we are impacted as well as how we create impact, and includes our relations with other people rather than limiting inquiry to humans versus the physical environment. Deep ecology is a spiritual study; not because the concepts are gathered from spiritual texts or teachings but because each and every concept aligns easily with the core tenets of every major spiritual path.

How we participate with one another and with our natural environment is largely determined by the decisions we make as individuals. This book brings deep ecology knowledge to bear on individual experience and the decisions that arise in and from individual experience without giving up the idea of membership in our various communities. It brings focus to the well-being of ourselves and others in a way that skirts the individualistic it's-all-about-me thinking that is predominant in current Western culture, and simultaneously illuminates the problems inherent in individualistic thinking.

I come to this topic as an occupational therapist and educator with grounding in occupational science, as well as the many theoretical frameworks that support occupational therapy processes. I should clarify here that occupational therapy is a health-care profession capable of serving anyone of any age who has difficulty participating in life due to disease, disability, or injustice. Occupational science, the body of knowledge that supports occupational therapy, is largely a study of how we can occupy ourselves in ways that support our participation in all that life offers.

I define *occupation* as what we do with our time that has meaning. Examples of occupations include the playing occupation of a two-year-old child; the rejuvenating occupation of a long walk for a tired office worker; the working occupation of a factory employee; and the learning occupation of a student. Supported by more than one hundred years of practice and three decades of formal scientific inquiry about occupation, a primary tenet of occupational therapy is that occupying ourselves with what holds meaning promotes well-being. In other words, when we are able to act on what holds meaning for us, our burdens feel less burdensome.

In this book, I rely on *An Occupational Perspective of Health* by Ann Wilcock and Clare Hocking for knowledge about the effects of occupation, and *The Meaning of Everyday Occupation* by Betty Risteen Hasselkus for evidence of where and how in our experiences meaning is a factor in our well-being. The focus on human experience in these volumes brings attention to the tangible perspective that demonstrates the significance of meaning in the quality, if not longevity, of our lives.

The intentional use of occupations can create a profound difference in our well-being. I have observed such changes in myself when I occupied myself based on what held meaning for me, and I have observed similar changes in many other people. I have wondered what kind of scientific knowledge might explain this phenomenon. Deep ecology seemed useful to this inquiry because it showed why many of my thoughtful decisions were ill-conceived and how they might have been more satisfactory had I known more about the qualities that sustain life.

Capra published an expansion of *The Web of Life* concepts in collaboration with biologist Pier Luigi Luisi in *The Systems View of Life: A Unifying Vision* volume. As is *The Web of Life*, *The Systems View of Life* is grounded in the many branches of science that have something to say about what sustains life, including human life. From these sciences emerge four qualities of primary importance. These qualities are detailed by Capra and Luisi with credit given to the scientists who made important relevant discoveries in their various fields of study. In the following chapters, I summarize those discoveries and translate the scientific terms into everyday language.

The four qualities that support human life are a good place to begin. I explain these briefly here and then dedicate a chapter of discussion to each quality. It is important to remember that none of the four qualities stands in isolation—all are intertwined, but the intertwining nature is so complex that to understand each quality it must be temporarily extracted from the rest to some degree. The forthcoming chapters attempt to isolate each quality for a close look and to identify how each is integrated with the others.

Chapter 1 describes the self-organizing pattern, which is the ability of a system, alive or not, to set its own pattern of organization. As chaos evolves, a system may reach a tipping point and move into a clear pattern of activity that is no longer chaotic but instead has some predictability. Norbert Wiener's descriptions of patterns and connections in his book *The Human Use of Human Beings: Cybernetics and Society* help us understand this phenomenon and its relevance to human experience in terms of patterns of activity and communication. Chapter 1 discusses how, in human experience, an individual with a self-organizing pattern appears somewhat predictable to others and therefore demonstrates some boundaries regarding how they will and will not interact with others. This chapter addresses how our habits, routines, and rituals are patterns that express our personality, and how our self-knowledge can also be described as a pattern that conveys our identity. I emphasize that the self-organizing pattern can be considered a basis for all transactions with others, and that the integrity of the self-organizing pattern is thus the foundation for the integrity in all transactions.

Chapter 2 breaks briefly from the listing of four qualities to explore the nuances of how a self-organizing pattern supports our ability to be in relationship with others, and simultaneously how lack of a self-organizing pattern diminishes our ability to connect with others. Although descriptions in this chapter are examples of human experience rather than descriptions of the qualities, they provide a perspective on the meaning implicit in maintaining a life-supporting, self-organizing pattern. These descriptions are supported by author Anne Wilson Schaef's explanations of addiction in *When Society Becomes an Addict*. I also discuss variants of hierarchical relationships and the importance of the self-organizing pattern in these. I show how socially constructed (inauthentic) hierarchies create social injustice situations, such as racism and other oppressive patterns, as well as some of the problematic dynamics implicit in the health-care model predominantly used in Western culture.

Chapter 3 is about the process of cognition from the perspective offered by biologists Humberto Maturana and Francisco Varela in *Autopoiesis and Cognition: The Realization of the Living*. Their view is a unique and challenging contribution that considers living systems (people) as self-contained (think self-organizing pattern) to the extent that their only point of actual reference for learning is their own self. I explain how we learn about the world *only* through what we already know, and how this makes new experiences and perspectives difficult to receive, much less to understand and incorporate into our thinking.

The proccess of cognition is all about learning, and that includes learning across many dimensions of our experience. I draw on multiple perspectives for an understanding of different dimensions of human experience and how they relate to one another. Piaget and his colleagues' child development model explained in *Intelligence and Affectivity: Their Relationship during Child Development* and in *The Psychology of the Child* and Stanislov Grof's findings about the subtler dimensions of experience described in *Beyond the Brain: Birth, Death, and Transcendence in Psychotherapy* anchor my explanation of the spectrum of dimensions of human experience. Between the two, the spectrum covers everything from the most tangible physical experience to the most unfathomable spiritual experience. Chapter 3 explains why the full spectrum of dimensions is important to how we maintain our self-organizing pattern in the face of stress.

Chapter 4 is about the dissipative structure. The word dissipate is generally interpreted as an indication of dispersion, or to represent the idea of falling apart, and is consistent with the traditional interpretation of the second law of thermodynamics in terms of a chaotic spindown that culminates in destruction of a life system. In this chapter, however, I describe physicist Ilya Prigogene and chemist Isabelle Stengers new interpretation of the second law of thermodynamics as it is described in *Order out of Chaos: Man's New Dialog with Nature*. I explain that sometimes when new information becomes available there is a tipping point that turns the entropic process around and, rather than overwhelming the life system even more, the new information allows reorganization of what was falling apart into a more viable pattern.

A dissipative structure is one that allows an ongoing process of disorganization and reorganization, so that the distress of disorganization is mitigated and so that learning—even evolution—can occur. Physicist and philosopher David Bohm's ideas about unfolding and enfolding meaning are introduced as a way to explain how our different dimensions of experience support one another through collaborative participation. I use his article directed toward scientists, "A New Theory of the Relationship of Mind and Matter" and his less technical book *Unfolding Meaning: A Weekend of Dialogue with David Bohm*, to support my explanations.

Chapter 4 explains how this is key to the mitigation of stress and how we use our internal resources to grow into new capacity in the face of increasingly difficult problems.

Chapter 5 expands on Bohm's ideas described in his article "A New Theory" about meaning beginning with a brief description of three properties of quantum physics and how these can be interpreted to describe human experience. I discuss the dilemma of our natural inclination to diminish the value of our more mundane experiences, and how by doing this we lose opportunities for profound spiritual experiences. I tie the meaning in how we occupy ourselves to raising our potential for spiritual experience and a sense of wholeness.

Chapter 6 invites readers to consider the qualities that support life when making decisions. Each quality, as well as the topic of relations and boundaries, is addressed individually with ideas to consider.

Life: What Is Sustainable and What Is Not

Every life is dependent on relationships. Every life form encompasses a smaller life form, from our human body down to our tiniest cells, and every life form is encompassed by a larger life form, from the tiniest cells all the way up to our global ecology. According to deep ecology scholars Fritjof Capra and Pier Luigi Luisi in *The Systems View of Life,* these layers are essentially a network of connections that support one another with links to what is smaller and what is bigger, as well as what is within the same level of life.

Within each layer, every component of the life form networks with other components. Each cell in a human body networks with other cells to make up and support the life form we call a tissue. Each cell, or component of the tissue, plays a part in keeping the tissue alive. Tissues network to form an organ, again with each component (tissue) of an organ playing a part in the health of that organ. As components of a human life, organs network together to support the human, with each organ playing its unique role. Humans in turn are components of a family, then a community, and so on up to the entire global ecology and beyond. Figure i is one way to picture this. The multiple cells that make up the tissue are included to give the idea of components working together. You can imagine also that there are many tissues that make up an organ, many organs that make up the human, and so on.

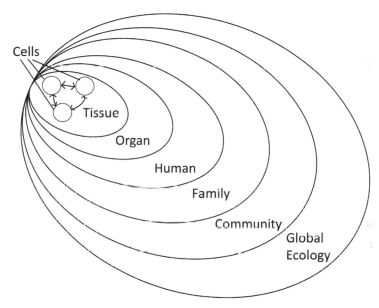

Figure i. Encompassed and Encompassing Life Systems.

Capra and Luisi tell us that every life system, be it a cell, a human, a community, or something else, must have a self-organizing pattern, a process of cognition, and a dissipative structure in order to stay alive. For humans—individuals and communities—the quality of meaning is added as a fourth necessity. They argue that how well these four qualities are supported determines the health of the life system.

With that understanding, let's now take a deeper look into each of the four qualities and the roles they play in human experience.

1 SELF-ORGANIZING PATTERN

Let's begin with a close look at what happens within a single unit of human life, because that is what we focus on every day. Capra and Luisi say that every life system, from a single cell to the global ecology, has components that are networked into some kind of pattern.[1] To build a visual representation that will display what is important, we begin with a circle, representative of a human, with triangles representing the components of a pattern of organization. Figure 1.1 shows this. For example, organs are components that together support a human life. To provide this support, they must support one other. And so it is: The heart beats, sending blood around to the liver and brain and lungs to nourish them. The lungs bring oxygen to the blood, which provides one kind of needed nourishment, and the liver cleanses the blood of toxins that might tarnish the ability of the brain and heart to do their jobs. In this way, each organ contributes to the maintenance of the others and therefore contributes to the well-being of the whole person.

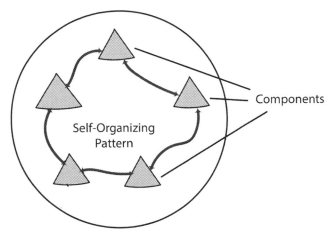

Figure 1.1. Self-Organizing Pattern.

First described by cyberneticists as a result of their study of feedback and self-regulation, the organizational ability to make decisions based on feedback was seen as a key characteristic of life.[2] Biologists Humberto Maturana and Francisco Varela weighed in with the importance of self-maintenance.[3] A successful self-organizing pattern requires each and every component to function well, even as the pattern guarantees support from other components so this can happen. A healthy human body is one with internal organs that function effectively and are sufficiently linked to make their contributions and to receive what they need. We can function with a pacemaker, but the need for one represents a vulnerability to certain kinds of activity. We can fill our lungs with toxins and still manage to work, play, love, and care for ourselves in other ways, but that toxic load will impact the ability of our liver to support other organs. When there is weakness or vulnerability in one organ, the entire life system becomes more vulnerable to stress because communications among the organs are weakened. And when nourishment and information can't be transmitted as effectively, the life system will more quickly fall into a state of observable illness, if not death.

Key to the intactness of components and communications is that the organizational pattern must be determined by the life system itself. All people need to have a certain degree of authority over what will or will not be included in their experience. When decisions are driven from within, they tend to prioritize choices that will meet their needs. Self-determination, internal locus of control, self-agency, and autonomy are all terms that demonstrate a self-organizing pattern. Maintaining an internal locus of control or self-agency positions us as a dependable entity with whom a relationship is possible. Even though we are unique, others know something about what to expect from us. But being unique is both what makes us valuable to others and what creates relational discord.

Let's look at the self-organizing pattern as it relates to uniqueness and relationships. Individualism is generally understood to be characterized by attending to one's needs and pursuing one's desires without much attention to how this might impact others. There is a distinct difference between individualism and maintaining a self-organizing pattern. The former carries an assumption that our individual needs must come first and that other people should jump in to help us when we can't manage ourselves. The latter also requires that one's own needs be attended first and foremost but assumes this can and will be managed internally. This sidesteps the need for others to behave in a certain way and leaves them free to create their own self-organizing pattern.

As we will see, individuals with self-organizing patterns change over time in response to others' words and behaviors, grow in their capacity to relate to others, and are increasingly able to contribute to their communities accordingly. In fact, many of the roles we play out through our habits, routines, and rituals are initially derived from what we see other people do. Contrarily, people who hold to individualism risk trampling on others, thus losing their options to make meaningful contributions and to grow in qualitative capacity.

Perhaps the most perplexing and paradoxical issue humans face is whether to pursue our own individualities or to opt for a greater sense of belonging. The incorporation of the four qualities described in this book creates a balance between meeting our needs for individuality and our need for belonging. We don't have to choose one or the other, though the incremental choices we make sometimes seem to do just that.

The physical balance we call upon to stand and walk is actually a dynamic of shifting our weight back and forth between the two sides of our bodies. In the process, our upper and lower torso also shift in relation to one another. Our trunks and hips pivot on each other so that left and right sides are always both active, and forward movement is facilitated. With the pivot, one leg swings forward in a walking motion. In much the same way, our individualities pivot on a sense of belonging, and vice versa, allowing us to step into new ways of doing and being, and new perspectives, as we move along. We actually become someone new with each step, and the four qualities that support life provide us with a path.

The self-organizing pattern maintains us by attending to our real needs, whereas individualism brings more focus to what we want. Although the conformity implicit in belonging is typically abhorred by individualists, adherence to that sentiment denies the possibility that conformity might carry its own meaning, and diminishes the possibility of the very connections with others that are critical to our own growth. Individualism without the balance of belonging, like trying to walk forward with only one leg, cannot take us very far, and belonging without a self-organizing pattern is a lethal prospect.

Habits, Routines, and Rituals

Rather than looking at human life as a set of functioning bodily organs, a different way to interpret the components of our organizational pattern is to think in terms of our daily experiences. For example, our habits and routines support each other and help us navigate the events we encounter—a morning coffee, a bedtime snuggle, or a walk with a friend can be pivotal to how the day goes. If we can't follow our normal routine, we may feel out of sorts all day. Each activity or sequence supports other activities. We rise in time for coffee. Like clockwork, we communicate with our friend about plans to walk. We organize our days so that the things we value can happen. Consequently, what we do with our time determines the degree of support we provide for our health and well-being.

Many occupational scientists have written about habits and routines.[4] The general consensus is that whereas habits are automatically repeated behaviors, routines are more complex behaviors that may include a sequence of functionally related habits. For example, people who value a healthy body might develop a routine of cooking from scratch. This routine requires certain habits related to shopping, kitchen maintenance, and time management. As another example, people who desire to spend time with a certain group of friends may develop a routine of going to certain gathering places and engaging in activities of shared interest. Habits that support this routine might include what route we choose as we move from one place to another, what clothes we wear, and how we organize our mealtimes.

Rituals may be routines also, but rituals tend to be more deliberate behaviors imbued with a higher degree of importance and are more readily included in spiritual narratives. Betty Hasselkus gives the example of caring for an ill or elderly loved one in a certain way that is protective of their health and well-being. Hygiene and mealtime care are mentioned, but in her descriptions we can see that the meaning of dignity and well-being, when applied to the mundane aspect of hygiene or mealtime experience, creates a different kind of satisfaction that can be interpreted as having a spiritual quality.[5] In my mind, any mundane habit can become a ritual, depending on attitude and intent. For example, daily exercise that appears to be a mundane physical event can be seen as a time to free the mind for reflection, spiritual contemplation, or to deepen a social connection to a spiritual level.

How we organize our time, what habits and routines we employ, and how we reorganize ourselves when something goes awry are critical to our well-being and to how well we can carry out the roles we've agreed to play in our families and communities. Perhaps more to the point, Norbert Wiener suggests that our ability to maintain a self-organizing pattern profoundly influences how long we will live and our quality of life for the duration.[6] Wiener's view is grounded in cybernetics, which integrates perspectives from many other fields including engineering, quantum physics, biology, social science, and mathematics. From this broad base of knowledge, he suggests that our ability to organize protects us from entropy in our environment and makes it possible for us to not only maintain ourselves but to evolve in spite of environmental chaos.

Communication and feedback can be either informational or material. Wiener reminds us that our physical body's homeostasis depends on many physiological feedback mechanisms that convey how our body is responding to changes. These feedback mechanisms trigger stabilizing adjustments in our physiology. Feedback in this context is material (e.g., hormones and neurotransmitters). Wiener also discusses human to human communication. He proposes that what we actually communicate is our pattern of organization, which we will soon see is equivalent to transmitting our identity.[7]

Human embodiment entails many operational patterns of organization in addition to homeostasis. Many if not all of these can be seen as potential ways to communicate our identity. For example, when we simply think about making a movement a communication loop is initiated between the brain and the body part we intend to move. The thought and the actual process of moving both stimulate neurons to fire in order to make the movement happen the way it was intended. The brain tells appropriate muscles what to do and the muscles tell the brain what they intend to do and, when action begins, what they are doing. If something goes awry, corrections are made in the communication loop so that the intended outcome will be more likely.

The movements we make support our intended actions and our actions tell other people something about who we are. At a more subtle level, too, our movements express our identity. Many people have had the experience of seeing someone from afar, too far away or at the wrong angle to discern facial features, yet the way that person moves is unique and can be recognized as belonging to one certain individual. Identity can be established based on just that.

In terms of our more conscious patterns, cybernetic principles speak to our use of time. As we proceed with a time-sensitive activity, ongoing communication and feedback between ourselves and our environment allows us to alter our activity according to the relation between our process and the amount of time available. When the time allotted for an activity turns out to be insufficient for the activity, we make decisions about whether we will continue the activity, discontinue the activity, or continue the activity in an altered way. Our habits and routines often factor heavily in these decisions.

According to Hasselkus, habits, routines, and rituals provide a structure for proceeding through our days and weeks that ensures the comfort of familiarity and gives us a role to play in our community. She describes how holding on to these patterns or developing new patterns in new situations can free us to think creatively or to ponder our unique identities as they relate to the situation at hand.[8] This kind of multidimensional approach to activities—doing the habits or routines or rituals while contemplating one's identity or role in the larger picture—sets up a kind of wholeness that can be more satisfying than simply carrying out a task. The deeper meanings of our actions can be brought to the fore in this kind of contemplation, and these meanings become the communicative connectors between our physical, social, mental, and spiritual dimensions. The doing typically involves the physical dimension of activity, and the contemplation of identity generally involves thinking. Together, our patterns of thinking and doing contribute to our identities, and our identities determine how we show up and participate in the world.

Identity

Two fairy tales, "Cinderella" and "Jack and the Beanstalk," respectively illustrate the lack of a self-organizing pattern and a successful self-organizing pattern. These stories also make clear that what people (or story characters) do is critical to our understanding of their identity.

In the traditional Cinderella story, Cinderella decides very little in terms of how her day goes. Her step-family's demands take precedence over any wish she might have regarding how she spends her time. When her wish to go to the royal ball is laughed at, she immediately stops pursuing the idea of going. She presumably has numerous homemaking skills, including enough skill to help her stepsisters with their gowns for the ball, but there are zero hints that she ever considers applying those skills to help herself. She takes at face value the edict that she cannot go and has little vision for herself beyond that. Her response is to dissolve into tears until a source outside herself, the fairy godmother, comes to rescue her and takes over the role of dressmaking that Cinderella could actually have participated in with some competence. When she gets to the ball, she again fails to organize herself by not keeping track of the time and yet again when she loses her shoe on her way out of the palace. One has to wonder how efficient or effective she could have been with a crown on her head.

Cinderella's identity is ambiguous. She is portrayed as a beautiful and deserving young lady in an unfair environment, yet she can't function outside that environment. Her real identity—the identity that would reflect her true capacities—is left out of the picture. Many young girls dream of being identified as beautiful and deserving: they dream Cinderella dreams. But the story of Cinderella gives no clues about how to achieve that status.

The truth is that how we organize ourselves—our self-organizing pattern—determines the characteristics of our identity and how we express ourselves through words, work, and play. And how we express ourselves determines, in large part, the kinds of relationships we are able to create and sustain. One has to wonder what Cinderella and the prince found to talk about and upon what common interests or values their ensuing relationship was based.

In "Jack and the Beanstalk," Jack is able to self-organize. He may make some decisions that others would not make, but at least they are decisions. At every turn in his story he plays an assertive role, taking care of himself and eventually also providing for his aging mother. He is portrayed as the kind of person who goes after what he wants, then wants to be left alone. He is willing to go out, make a trade with a stranger, climb the beanstalk, talk with the giants, and then trick them. Although his way of doing things does not seem to leave much room for building relationships with others, I don't doubt for a minute that he could have found something to say were he in Cinderella's slippers at the ball. His way of organizing himself includes an openness to conversation and negotiations.

On the other hand, would Cinderella have ever climbed that beanstalk? Would she have knocked on the giant's door? No, she would have lost her shoe making the climb, mistimed her escape from the giant's house, and been boiled for dinner.

Cinderella and Jack each have a unique identity that was informed by their respective experiences, yet Cinderella's identity leaves many questions about who she really is. Her habits and routines were not selected by her, nor did her role in her home give her opportunities to make other choices. On the other hand, Jack's identity is pretty clear, as were his choices. We know we can expect him to take care of himself and that he can and will find helpful resources along his way. There is much more to be said about this, because our identity has a lot do with our ability to network socially, and this also is crucial to our ability to stay alive.

Whereas the narrative of fairy tales is usually fairly straightforward, maintaining a self-organizing pattern in real life is not necessarily simple or easy. It sometimes means giving up something that has been previously sought out in order to remain true to oneself. Ruby Hamad writes about a Black woman named Danai, described as a very friendly woman initially, who learned to avoid attempting friendships with her coworkers because of the racism she experienced on a daily basis in her workplace. When she reached the end of her maternity leave, she chose to resign rather than return to that oppressive environment.[9] She traded the opportunity to develop her professional capacity for time to follow the work of activists and writers whose perceptions and perspectives validated her own and whose work supported her identity as a Black woman.

The occupations we participate in provide a way of knowing ourselves better.[10] Every action is potentially followed by feedback, as is every instance of self-expression. This feedback informs us of the messages we have sent. If we pay attention, we can learn about ourselves through our interactions because these either affirm who we are or raise questions about our identity, our roles, and how we fit in.

When Danai found that she did not fit in socially with her peers at work, she chose a different occupation that at the outset seems more isolating, but which in fact helped her feel validated—bringing a sense of belonging in a different community. Her decision to engage in the occupation that at the very least affirmed her identity as a Black woman reflects a self-organizing pattern sufficient to support her emotional and intellectual needs. It also set the stage for more satisfying social relationships.[11]

Regardless of what we include in our lives, whether it is coffee or meditation, bowling or social action, risky or cautious behavior, what we choose to do informs how we see ourselves and how others see us. This is one way to look at our identity. The choices we make place us in specific roles that structure and inform our interactions. If we spend time in a workplace, we are an employee or a boss or a coworker. If we choose to marry, we are a partner. If we choose to raise children, we are a parent or caregiver. The experiences we garner as we play out our roles inform who we are and support who we become.

Those experiences are contained in our memories in terms of the content of events that occurred, our interpretation of those events, and how we responded. Memories also remind us about the challenges we have faced and thus inform our future decisions. How we responded in the past tells us about our patterns of reaction and response and our capacity to participate. Our interpretation of any event informs us about how that event fits into the overall pattern of our experiences. More to the point of my theme in this book, our interpretation of any event informs our ability and inclination to reach for either the life-supporting potential or the life-denying potential available in that event. Altogether, the many facets of experience tell us who we are.

Some people who grow up in the city identify themselves as city people, while others despise city life because they did not resonate well with events that happened there. Success in navigating city life, built on many experiences of doing just that, creates (or doesn't) confidence in one's ability to navigate, to understand and follow traffic rules, and to engage with others in a way that is expected, if not appreciated. More important than specific skills, though, is the knowledge of what we know how to do and what we don't know how to do. No matter what experiences we have had, recognizing where the gaps are in our self-knowledge allows us to move ahead with confidence or to move more carefully when that is warranted. Self-knowledge goes hand-in-hand with identity, and both are important to how we conduct our relationships.

Self-Knowledge

Self-knowledge is not inevitable. With every new experience, what we know about ourselves is disrupted to some degree by the new information embedded in our response to the new event. How I respond to observing a traumatic event tells me something about myself. How I respond to an unexpected visit from a relative tells me something about myself. In either case—in every case—what I learn may be as much a surprise to me as the event itself. The bigger the surprise, the more difficult it can be to include that new information in my understanding of who I am. That means the connections in my pattern of organization will be compromised. I won't be able to function as efficiently or as effectively as I did before until those connections are rebuilt to include the new information. This kind of rebuilding is what a dissipative structure allows. We will look at that more closely in chapter 4.

But now let us look closer at how self-knowledge is constructed. Let's consider that it might be comprised of three components that work together to support one another and to support our overall knowledge of ourselves. We can use the same image of a pattern of organization for this thought experiment although our self-knowledge is not a life system in and of itself. Figure 1.2 shows the three components of self-knowledge as acceptance of feelings, accurate information, and clear thinking, all supporting one another in the circle at the left in figure 1.2, with the effects of a breach derailing the mutual support of these components at the right.

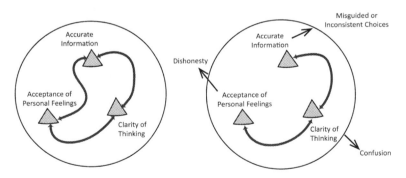

Figure 1.2. Self-Knowledge.

We can see that issues in any of the three components will reduce the integrity of the other two. If we do not accept our feelings about a situation, it will be more difficult to obtain and use accurate information and to think clearly. What we say to others will not be consistent. We may appear dishonest, whether or not we intend dishonesty. If we do not have accurate information, we cannot possibly think clearly, and our feelings will be skewed according to our perceptions, perhaps blown out of proportion. Our choices will be misguided. If we are not thinking clearly, our confusion will affect our ability to process emotions and to identify accurate information. Our confusion may spread to other susceptible people as we engage with them.

Maintaining internal coherency is an ongoing self-care project. It requires constant attention, and when we miss a beat, we put ourselves and others at risk. The gap created not only makes us vulnerable, it diminishes our ability to communicate effectively and to establish or maintain satisfying relationships. It may also cause us to harm others. Our confusion can make it more difficult for others to function efficiently because they are denied clear and accurate information about what we think or need. Our lack of acceptance (and perhaps awareness) of our own feelings means others will not know what to expect from us or whether they can trust us, even as we believe we are being honest and trustworthy! Our inaccurate beliefs and misguided speech or actions can, and sometimes do, diminish other individuals' ability to live freely and productively. On the other hand, when we choose to care for ourselves by attending to gaps in our self-knowledge as they arise to a level of awareness, we position ourselves to participate in relationships that function well and feel satisfying. All this becomes apparent when we look closely at self-organization in the context of relationships, which we will do in chapter 2.

Key Points

- Every single experience we have provides an opportunity to choose a life-sustaining path or a path that does not support the four qualities we need in order to thrive.
- Everyone has components (experiences) that make up the unique pattern of their identity and capacity and those components must be linked in some way in order to work as a unit.

- A self-organizing pattern requires ongoing maintenance that keeps our identity up to date as we evolve and provides an ongoing, solid basis for relationship with others.
- What we choose to do in terms of habits, routines, and rituals provides experiences that make up how we see ourselves and how others see us.
- Every single experience we have has potential to teach us about ourselves, if we pay attention.
- Self-knowledge is comprised of acceptance of feelings, accurate information, and clear thinking, which work together to support our ability to communicate clearly.

2 RELATIONSHIPS AND BOUNDARIES

We have seen that our self-organizing pattern is the basis of our identity. We will see in chapter 3 that our process of cognition allows us to build our identity as well as our capacity to solve problems. The structure of our being, our dissipative structure (see chapter 4), supports these patterns and processes. But for what purpose?

One distinct purpose is to support our very life. We need food and shelter and these, plus so much more, are made available through our relationships and interactions with other people.[1] For many Indigenous people culture and community are integral to healing and thus to life itself.[2] To be in community requires relationships. Though self-organizing patterns may occur in non-living systems, the possibility of relationship in human experience, where learning and mitigation of stress is possible, is steeped with meaning that makes us feel very much alive. The quality of meaning (chapter 5), which is embedded in and drives our relation with others, holds it all together.

No matter what we do, there are ongoing transactions between ourselves and the people and world around us. These transactions occur no matter how we occupy ourselves. It is through them that we gather nourishment and make our contributions. Transactions also hold potential for harm.[3] Some habits, for example, support us in some ways yet harm us in other ways; we would not eat things that are not nourishing or imbibe in harmful substances if this were not so. Similarly, some habits and routines support healthy relationships, and some are harmful to our relationships and to the people with whom we interact. For example, a habit of going along with what others say in order to stay in their good graces not only denies one's own needs but donates power to others that is unnecessary and burdensome.[4] The donation of personal power is a boundary breach that places us at risk. Because the flipside of the self-organizing pattern coin is our boundaries, in order to more fully understand our patterns and our identity, we need to take a good look at boundaries.

Boundaries

The idea of relational boundaries is complicated. On one hand, there is a relationship that is all about being and doing things together. On the other hand, boundaries suggest limits on such togetherness. It is easy to see how physical boundaries factor into the patterns we set. We all make choices about what we will or won't eat, or touch, or do—particularly in the case of high-risk behaviors. Everyone sets their own boundaries based on their preferences and what they know about their capacity.

Social boundaries function similarly. As we learn about our capacity to participate safely and successfully in transactions with others, we reset our boundaries on with whom we will engage and with whom we will not engage. For example, we set limits on who touches us, and when and how, and we do so via how we manage ourselves. It may not be a problem to be bumped while standing in line at the grocery because we have a choice to move away. It is more complicated when a boss lays a too-friendly hand on our shoulder because we may not feel we are free to move away without complicating consequences. Likewise, when a friend pushes us (figuratively speaking) to do something we don't want to do, we might choose to refuse. If the friend tricks us into participating, we may choose to set a new boundary that will provide us with better protection.

These subtle boundaries are all about how we organize ourselves. We may choose to stay beyond the reach of people who can't keep their hands to themselves by changing our route to the coffee pot at work. We may choose to spend less time with those who have manipulated or coerced us to do something we didn't want to do. Changing our habits protects us from harm without being disrespectful to or infringing upon others.

Organizing ourselves according to our self-knowledge rather than according to what others think or do is key to building potential for satisfying experiences. This is core to many nuances of relational boundaries. We've looked at the self-organizing pattern in terms of our identity and our ability to express ourselves clearly. If boundaries are truly the flipside of that coin, it might be useful to consider boundaries in those terms too.

Boundaries around Identity

Regardless of how others define us, if we have been paying attention, we know better than anyone else who we are and what our capacity is because we have more information about ourselves than anyone else. It is *our* experience that makes us who we are. Although another's view of us may be interesting or even valuable at times, good boundaries will not allow the opinions of others to define us or what we are capable of doing.

In addition to maintaining our integrity, good boundaries are essential to our ability to expand our capacity. As we set and reset our boundaries to navigate different experiences, we evolve into a clearer image of who we are, what we need, and what we can tolerate as we open to new learning. This process requires reflection and an understanding of other members of our community as well as of the community itself. The practice of using reflection to map our process and progress builds capacity beyond logical thinking. As we will see, building the kind of pattern where more than one kind of thinking is incorporated feeds into our process of cognition and supports our ability to mitigate stress. It energizes us to move forward as the meaning of what we are doing plays out. So boundaries are not only a safeguard against problems, they contribute to our ability to solve problems we are not yet aware of and direct our focus to do what we really need to do!

Just as others can never see the complete picture of who we are, we can never know the full picture of another person's identity and capacity. Noting some characteristics and capacities of another may help us in our interactions, but it is important to remember that there is always more that we are not able to see. Although it is easy to reach for security by constructing a narrative that we've only partially seen or heard it would be unfair to settle upon a single interpretation as the whole truth about another person. Doing so violates the boundaries of the other by imposing so-called truths while shutting down the possibility of more accurate and complete understanding.

Assumptions about other people also hinders our own ability to move forward with clarity. However, limiting our assumptions about others frees us to take what they say and do at face value, and we free them to evolve as they express themselves. Placing a boundary on our assumptions thus allows us the grace to not know everything while honoring our direct experience of what others say and do.

Boundaries around Self-Expression

I use the term self-expression broadly here to include what we say and how we act. Figure 2.1 shows a relationship between two people who have well-developed self-organizing patterns and therefore have appropriate boundaries. In this kind of exchange, each person speaks from personal self-knowledge, based on his or her lived experience, rather than talking about another's experience. It is hard enough to understand our own experience, much less to understand the events in another's life. It is better to let others explain themselves, and it is better to explain our own perspective so that it can be expressed clearly and as completely as we wish without taking the risk that we will be misrepresented. In this way, we make no assumptions and step on no toes. We have a better chance to be heard. Neither person is put at risk because both speak only from their own experience. No boundaries are breached and both parties benefit.

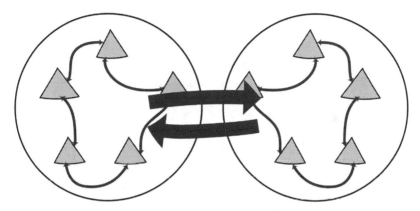

Figure 2.1. Clear Communications between Two Self-Organizing Individuals.

Speaking our own truth enables self-reliance and exempts us from dependency on what others think. It also releases them from any need to please us. Instead, we come to rely primarily on what we can do to make ourselves feel safe and satisfied. Whether others please us or not will be immaterial. We will be able to respond with integrity no matter what happens.

At the opposite end of the spectrum of being pleased is being harmed. It does matter if harm is done, and an appropriate response is to set different boundaries. When our boundaries are healthy enough to support clear expression of who we are and also to prevent harm, what others do or say will be of little consequence.

With good boundaries, we will, as much as possible and based on our self-knowledge, determine to what extent we will participate in any given experience. When circumstance or choice places us in a difficult situation, we can choose either to react automatically or to participate more fully in the course of a thoughtful response. We can also choose to participate as an observer to a greater or lesser degree. Darnella Frazier, the young woman who filmed George Floyd's murder in 2020, chose to participate with a thoughtful response not just as an observer but as a responsible observer—a witness willing to act upon what she saw by sharing it. With this choice, her participation made a profound difference for many people. Her example shows how our choices about the extent to which we will participate can be simplistic or complex, blending a range of dimensions of experience in one act. We will investigate this more in chapters 4 and 5 because the participation in and through multiple dimensions of experience in how we occupy ourselves absolutely *is* one of the most powerful ways we take care of ourselves and those around us. And all that rests on the boundaries we enact.

As suggested above, it is impossible to avoid experiences generated by other people, including those that are disruptive to our own patterns and processes. New events, especially unexpected events, raise a need for reassessment and a potential shift of the lines we've drawn in our patterns. As we set and reset our boundaries, we evolve into a clearer expression of who we are. But even when our identity shines, we may step on the toes of others just as their expressions might step on ours. These transactions are opportunities to know ourselves better. However, in order for self-knowledge to expand, transactions must be relatively safe. Safety can be found in boundaries, and boundaries are implicit in healthy relationships. And those, once we know what supports them, are a choice.

Let's go back to the idea that our triangles are experiential components rather than representative of components of self-knowledge. Imagine that the pattern in one of the circles in figure 2.1 has been disrupted. Something new has happened, and that experience is too fresh to have been processed and incorporated into the pattern. Perhaps that person had some profound changes in their life and haven't yet sorted out what it all means. The resulting disruption to their pattern of organization will impact everything they do.

Figure 2.2 shows the effect a poorly formed self-organizing pattern can have on our relationships. In this depiction, neither person has a self-organizing pattern, and both are at risk for boundary breaches coming and going. Let's say the person on the right begins the exchange with gaps in their self-knowledge. (We all do this frequently.) The person on the left disrupts their own pattern in an attempt to fill the gap the person on the right is demonstrating. But this intention to help can be problematic. For example, sometimes the gaps we think we see in others are really just our own unresolved issues projected, and the other person is actually doing very well! Furthermore, the help offered may not be desired or useful. It may be downright upsetting. Offering help in these situations is neither productive nor healthy for several reasons.

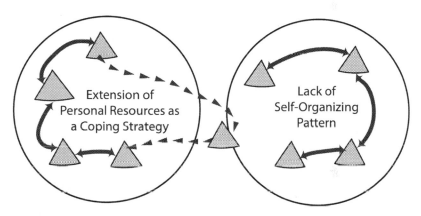

Figure 2.2. Disrupted Pattern Dynamics.

When we disrupt our own pattern of organization to help another, we make ourselves vulnerable because there will be no one "at home" to notice, much less to take care of our own needs. Healthy helping can only be achieved if we can help without compromising ourselves. Second, our efforts to help can create further disruption to the other person. We cannot possibly know what is truly best for someone else. There is a very real possibility that our best efforts will be misguided and will add more chaos, interfering with the other person's ability to develop his or her own pattern of organization. Furthermore, the interference can be perceived as intrusive or manipulative. If this occurs, communication will likely break down, first because clarity is compromised and second because the one who feels intruded upon may justifiably raise a defensive barrier to further communications.

Disruptions to our pattern of organization and relationships can also be experienced when someone says or does something that doesn't fit our perception of how the world should be. An unexpected action by someone close to us might interfere with the routine we were counting on completing, and suddenly our pattern of behavior is interrupted. The link between our activities is broken as new tasks require attention. A clumsy moment, such as spilling a drink or stubbing a toe, can do the same. Witnessing a traumatic event or a burst of emotion can also be disruptive. We are suddenly faced with a decision of how to respond. Our own emotions may be triggered in the process, and this may determine what we choose to do. In the mental dimension, learning a fact that doesn't fit easily into our belief system can be disruptive. It takes time to sort through how to fit new information into our understanding of the world.

It is clear that we can be disrupted by any of a variety of experiences. Going back to our interpretation of a pattern of organization as representative of different dimensions of our experience it becomes apparent that a disruption in any dimension—be it physical, social, emotional, mental, or other—can disturb our overall sense of balance. Positive experiences, too, can be as disruptive as experiences that are less desirable.[5] As we have seen, feelings that are unprocessed can diminish our ability to express ourselves clearly and with accuracy, and this becomes problematic in our relationships.

No matter what they say or do, whether they are clear or unclear, people around us will impact us, sometimes in a way that makes us uncomfortable. Likewise, no matter how careful we are, what we say and do impacts others, sometimes in a way that makes them uncomfortable. Learning in the mental operations realm is logical and therefore has a quality of consistency that makes learning mental operations a trustworthy guide. Emotions, on the other hand, come and go like the tide, and social and cultural norms can vary from person to person and from one group to another. Differences that cannot be easily accommodated are often problematic and painful. In our discussion of mitigating stress in chapter 4, we will look at how our thoughts and emotions can be linked to help us to move forward from an uncomfortable spot.

Hasselkus emphasizes that although these disruptions to the way we think the world should be may be uncomfortable, they can lead us to a better understanding of who we are even as we come to understand others.[6] Although discomfort can be intimidating, knowing who we are protects us from the fear of being overwhelmed by those differences. Well-formed boundaries affirm our authentic selves even as we open to deeper and more complex interactions with those who are different. In this way, it is possible that differences expressed by others can contribute to further development of our identity and boundaries while enriching our understanding of others, and without engaging in cultural appropriation. It is also possible that a need for uniformity or control might drive resistance to such learning.

Dependency and Addiction

It should be clear by now that lack of good boundaries is a common characteristic in people who have trouble developing or maintaining a self-organizing pattern. Dependency and addiction are perhaps the most obvious exemplars of this. The need for external stability lends itself to forming patterns of dependency. Of course, dependency is appropriate for those who are not yet adults, or who are incapable of making sound decisions due to illness or disability. Even so, those with less capacity must be given opportunities to make choices that are within the range of what they can do and they must have opportunities to develop new capacities. Feeling in charge of one's experience adds meaning to participation, and as we shall see, this extends life itself.

Unfortunately, patterns of dependency that develop when we are young often continue to hold us captive even after we acquire self-agency in some arenas of life. Dependency and independency are not exclusive of one another. An individual can sustain a self-organizing pattern in some aspects of his or her life, yet in other aspects, doing so does not come easily.

For example, we may learn as young children that a romantic relationship is more important than self-agency, or that it is the road to fulfillment (the Cinderella story). This might lead us to base decisions on our perception of what a potential partner would like rather than on our own authentic needs or desires. But this is characteristic of codependency and does not support healthy relationships.[7] Even if the same person is able to develop competency and self-agency in other areas of his or her life, developing that one aspect of self-agency does not solve the entire problem. Instead, it suggests that further risk is possible. For example, self-agency in the workplace and lack of self-agency in relationships can result in workaholic behaviors and relationship troubles within the workplace.

In another boundary breaching nuance, adults who have not learned to self-organize often fall into patterns of trying to control the behavior or expressions of others in order to give themselves a sense of security.[8] "If only" thoughts that indicate a desire for the world to be different without investing in personal change is one example of how this can play out. The extension of if-only thoughts are "should" statements. For example, we might say another person should do x, y, or z because that will improve the situation in some way. The problem with this is that the person saying "should" does not have enough insight to know what is good for someone else, and if they overreach in an to attempt to gain that insight, they will probably leave their own self behind: unembodied, unattended, and vulnerable.

Sometimes people who lack the ability to self-organize rely too much on what others do or say, without considering their own values or needs. This way of managing oneself fits Ann Wilson Schaef's descriptions of addiction[9] and codependency[10]. In the examples given above about relational dynamics where the lack of a self-organizing pattern exists, descriptors align with Schaef's list of addiction and codependency characteristics. Readers will also recognize that the qualities on Schaef's list—dishonesty, control, external referenting (finding more meaning in another's views than in one's own), dependency, fear, and loss of personal morality—are all relevant to the lack of a self-organizing pattern. It is easy to make the case that every characteristic Schaef mentions is rooted in lack of self-organization.

At the core of that argument is the fact that addictions are inherently deadly, and an ability to self-organize is required for life to continue. More bluntly put, it is impossible to engage in addictive behaviors and simultaneously support one's life. Indeed, failure to maintain a self-organizing pattern (and supporting boundaries) can have serious and long-term consequences for one's own life and for others with whom one engages.

Just as addictions and dependency can be traced to lack of a self-organizing pattern, domestic abuse; child abuse; racial, class, gender, disability discrimination and other injustices; and other behaviors that limit another individual's potential to participate fully and with autonomy can also be traced to lack of a self-organizing pattern on the part of the perpetrator. These are, in a nutshell, all attempts to amass power rather than taking time to look at one's own capacity honestly and building one's capacity by increasing self-knowledge. The outcome of those attempts to amass power always includes a boundary violation.

Particularly troubling is that when patterns of behavior lacking a self-organizing quality are culturally legitimized, they take on a larger inference of rightness, whether or not they are healthy. Scholars point out that while slavery was harmful to many people prior to the colonization of America, transatlantic slavery ushered in a way of doing and being that entrenched the idea of owning other humans into the identities of European-descent (White) Southerners if not White people across the nation.[11] In cultures where individualism is highly valued, one's identity takes on a sense of entitlement that is rarely yielded easily.

Indeed, that culturally legitimized inference of rightness continues to carry meaning in the current century in how White people identify themselves in relation to Black, Indigenous, and other people of color.

Prior to the transatlantic slave trade, Kendi explains in *Stamped from the Beginning*, the immoral nature of slavery was explained away by Portuguese royalty with the narrative that enslavers were saving the souls of those less fortunate. In reality the narrative was a marketing tool designed to stay in the good graces of the Pope and other religious entities.[12] The lie about motivation in slave-trading suggests a lack of ability to self-organize—that is, to be able to maintain oneself while respecting others need to do so also.

In current times, we see a continuation of that lack of self-organization and the missionary theme in the frequent inclination of White people to give unsolicited aid or advice to people who are not of European descent. In both past and present patterns of interaction White people disrupt efforts of Black, Indigenous, and other people of color to create and maintain their own self-organizing patterns. The culturally legitimized inference of White rightness continues to be problematic because the underlying self-organizing pattern issue at the cultural level has not been resolved.

Using this lens of what actually supports life reveals that a power grab based on oppression of others (disallowing their need to self-organize) does not constitute authentic authority and is not supportive of the lives of *anyone,* even though it appears to support power-holders. Joseph Campbell argued that what people are really looking for is a way to *feel* alive.[13] I would add that power grabs, such as the enactment of racist ideas and other kinds of abuse and discrimination, are all attempts to feel alive, and that there is always an addictive quality to these attempts that carries a lethal message.

All forms of reliance on external factors to fill gaps in one's pattern of organization have addictive qualities. This is different from accessing nourishment because nourishment supports the development of our capacity as physical, emotional, mental, and spiritual beings without inherently impacting others. Attempting to fill our own organizational gaps with the capacity of others, however, does inherently impact other people, and does so in a harmful way. In *When Society Becomes and*

Addict, Schaef masterfully details this problem in her demonstration that various characteristics of addiction are common patterns in our society. Her suggestion that these patterns are lethal is corroborated by what science tells us about sustaining life as well as by descriptions of the lived experience of Black, Indigenous, and other people of color.

The word oppression is generally understood to mean an unjust or cruel use of authority that is experienced as an undue weight that limits the ability of the oppressed to move about freely or to self-organize. Boundary issues do not necessarily suggest oppression, but oppression always implies boundary issues. The difference lies in how authority is used and in the longevity of the situation. People with legitimate authority can and should set or help set appropriate boundaries for those in their care. This is not oppression if the authority figure maintains a self-organizing pattern and creates a context in which those in their care can do likewise. We will look at hierarchical relations and different kinds of authority later in this chapter.

For some people, oppression resulting from one aspect of their identity may spur participation in oppressing others wherever privilege can be leveraged.[14] White women, historically oppressed by White men, play a significant part in the oppression of Black, Indigenous, and other people of color, perhaps because this is one of their few opportunities to feel powerful. Poor White men who are oppressed due to classist thinking might also leverage their privilege over women and Black, Indigenous, and other people of color as a way to feel better about themselves.

Indeed, elite White men manufactured this dynamic so that they would be assured of not losing their economic power.[15] In terms of the science that supports life, elite White men's overreliance on money prompted them to manipulate, through campaigns of disinformation, the thought processes of poor White people, pretending alliance through skin color while dismissing the need for respectful boundaries and withholding economic power. Tragically, the meaning of that guiding overreliance on money, at least in Western culture, continues to be prioritized over the more life-sustaining meaning of good boundaries, clear communications, and respectful connections among all community members that would foster mutual support.

The victim-persecutor-savior triangle is discussed widely in psychology literature. Moving from one to another role can happen in a heartbeat in any situation. When cultural standards and patterns support the lack of awareness and subsequent bad behavior inherent in that triangle, changing the experience of victimhood or persecution is all the more difficult. The answer is clearly not to move into the savior position (e.g., White men inciting violence to "save" White women who cry, White women developing programs to "save" Black, Indigenous, and other people of color). It would be better for everyone if efforts to change those dynamics were focused on bolstering one's own authentic power through development of the self-knowledge and self-determination inherent in a self-organizing pattern, and simply being respectful of others. Although this may seem counterintuitive in terms of community health, it is grounded in what science tells us will keep us, as individuals and as communities, alive.

Many people believe that racial or class or gender discrimination is primarily rooted in lack of understanding of the capacity of the "other." I have no doubt that that is a factor. However, I argue that no matter what is our understanding of another's capacity, discomfort in and a need to *manage* those relationships usually, if not always, is rooted in a lack of trust in our own ability to respond as we engage with someone who has differences, be that skin color, gender, cultural expectations, degree of ability to move or think, or a different level of emotional candor.

Individuals who can maintain their self-organizing pattern will have authentic power within easy reach. They will be able to cooperate with others and find new ways to meet their own needs when resources fall short. They will be able to encounter tragedy or joy and recover from both with relative ease. And depending on context and content, self-organizing individuals will also able to guide others without losing their own footing.

Hierarchical relations that demonstrate such self-organization on the part of those in authority are important for several reasons. Let's look first at that, and then come back to some of the problems generated by the misappropriation of power and complications where the one in power lacks an intact self-organizing pattern.

Hierarchical Relationships

Recall that in encompassing life systems, each human is encompassed by a family, an extended family, a community, and so on. The larger and more complex family, community, and cultural group impresses certain knowledge and values on the individual, and the individual has opportunities to make unique contributions to the identity and capacity of those groups. Communication must run both ways in order for this to happen. Healthy hierarchical relationships make these bilateral communications possible.

Hierarchical relations appear in nearly every aspect of our lives. Although some cultures and communities minimize this feature or distribute it among community members, there are always those who carry more authority because they have some kind of greater capacity. These individuals might serve as representatives of those with less capacity by providing them with an introduction to the larger group. The larger group can then welcome, nurture, and benefit from budding talents. Figures of authority might also guide those with less capacity by communicating what will and will not work in the larger community, or what is needed or desired by the larger community. In some cases, they set the guidelines, and at other times they serve as a conduit for resources, so all in their care will have what they need.

As those with lesser capacity feel appreciated and included in resource distribution, a sense of belonging develops, and with that comes a desire to participate more fully, to contribute, and to follow many if not all rules of play. But this is all dependent on their link to the larger community—the figure of authority through which their connection to the larger group is sustained. In other words, the representatives of the larger group carry at least some responsibility for the degree to which those in their care can experience a sense of belonging.

There are two aspects to hierarchical relations that beg consideration. The first is that when a person with greater capacity is in relationship with a person with lesser capacity, the former has, in geometrical proportions, a substantial influence on the life of the latter. Figure 2.3 shows the geometric proportions and the overlapping influence of a hierarchical relationship. We can imagine the two circles overlapping to a lesser or greater degree, and, respectively, less or more lines of communication between their patterns of organization.

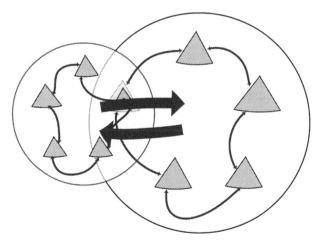

Figure 2.3. Relations with Authority.

What occurs between parent and child or any other version of a hierarchical relationship means more to the one who is dependent than it does to one with more authority. The parent may be a young child's whole world in a very literal sense. Although a parent may claim her world revolves around her child—and in one sense it may—the parent very necessarily has relationships with other adults because they are sources of access to food and shelter. The child eventually grows into greater independence and a need for other relationships. Until that happens, though, they are profoundly affected by every habit and routine, every pattern of doing and being that is demonstrated by their primary caregiver.

These patterns are deeply etched into a budding worldview that will last a lifetime, complete with a vision of that individual's own place in that worldview. In order for the child to live into those actual and projected roles, parents are responsible for guiding that preparation, introducing the child to more and more of the larger community, showing children how to participate, and giving them opportunities to do so. In other contexts, a boss, a teacher, a spiritual leader, or a mentor carry similar responsibilities.

In figure 2.3, both people represented demonstrate a self-organizing pattern. They are able to communicate clearly and directly with one another regardless of the fact that one has greater capacity. They are able to express their unique identities and to coordinate the roles they play while in transaction with one another. They are both able to manage themselves in a way that is respectful toward the other even when differences arise. The one with more capacity has opportunities to share knowledge and skill, and the one with less capacity has opportunities to learn and benefit from the resources available in and through the other. In the transaction, both are changed, so that the one with more capacity also learns.

But what happens when a figure of authority is ill prepared, perhaps unable to muster or maintain his or her own self-organizing pattern? When this happens, the model for a self-organizing pattern is incomplete, and the one who needs to learn this skill will be misguided into ways of doing and being that do not support life. In the context of family, a child might learn that relationships with others are confusing and difficult, if not fraught with disrespect, and that authority figures cannot be trusted. It is easy to see that these unfortunate lessons can translate into many problems for the child going forward. So the authenticity of power—the ability to maintain a self-organizing pattern—in the one with authority is essential to sustaining a viable and flourishing family or community.

Some designations of authority occur naturally due to differences in stages of development, while other designations are a result of someone having more experience or expertise in a particular arena. Having greater capacity suggests that a self-organizing pattern has been and is accomplished because one must reorganize one's patterns of thinking in order to accommodate new information. Authentic authority is evidenced when an individual demonstrates their capacity to the extent that others look to them as a role model or guide *and* when they are able to sustain themselves as well as care for those who look to them.

Figure 2.4 shows the encompassing social arenas, some individuals within them, and the connections among them that hinge on those individuals with greater capacity. The heavier lines of connection show lines of authority. In this figure we can imagine the authority figure with greater capacity coaxing or pulling those who depend on them into participation in the larger communities.

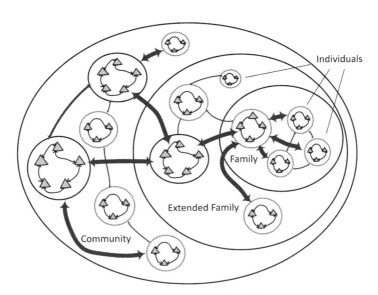

Figure 2.4. Encompassing Social Arenas.

This is the role of a parent, teacher, mentor, spiritual guide, and some workplace bosses—to build more capacity in those who have less so the community can meet new challenges and survive even as older and more accomplished members are no longer able to participate as frequently or as fully as they did. But to be sustainable, all relationships must be conducted with respectfulness and consideration of everyone's need to for self-agency.

The alternating pattern I described earlier regarding rotation of the human body as one walks forward, where both sides of the trunk are active and alternate taking the lead is applicable here too. It's not just a balance between community and individual. The same balance is exemplified in the relations between an authority figure and those under their authority. Parents allow their child—including babies—to lead at times. They respond to communications from the child about what the child needs. Then they take the lead to provide activities or sleep or food, watching to see what works for the child and what does not, always with a secondary goal of developing independence in the child. Good parenting is not coercive or controlling—it sets boundaries within which the child can find authentic ways of being and doing.

These early hierarchical relationships are at the root of every person's core pattern of organization. We also, at least in Western culture, rely on hierarchical relations through adulthood. A boss at work, a teacher, a leader of a religious group, government leaders, and others play a role similar to that played by parents in that they foster the development of new skills in those in their care. Mutually clear communications among those who are in positions of authority and those who are not is what makes it all viable.

PATRICIA GAILEY, PH.D.

Authentic Authority versus Socially Constructed Authority

We've just seen that some hierarchical relations are designated intuitively according to capacity. Others, however, are assigned for social reasons rather than the presence of greater capacity.

Socially Constructed Authority

Authority is sometimes conferred because either capacity or the potential for capacity is assumed. People can rise to positions of authority prior to expansion of their ability—many first-time parents know this all too well—and capacity can expand as new challenges are met.

But experience that is expected to build capacity can unfortunately be traversed without learning. One example is parenting experience that is so steeped in addictive practices that the possibility of good communication between parent and child is not possible. Another example is longevity in corporate employment that has not included curiosity about the complexity or nuances of decisions made by company bosses. The worker may have been exposed to the corporate ways of being and doing for many years, but if that worker is not paying attention, then the capacity for decision-making based on corporate culture will not develop.

When figures of authority do not understand what actually supports the lives of individuals and the life of the community, decisions about who will sit in a seat of power are made based on other criteria—social prowess, financial gain, family ties, longevity, or political gain. A quick analysis of these criteria strongly suggests they are more relevant to maintaining power and control than to maintaining the well-being of the community. Unfortunately, what takes a backseat are developments of new and valuable talents and making sure group members' needs are met. As a result, the entire community's ability to solve increasingly complex problems is diminished. As we will see later, the meaning implied in such appointments is quite superficial when stacked against the meaning of life and death. Socially constructed authority, therefore, is problematic from beginning to end.

An individual in a position of socially constructed authority may or may not enjoy a self-organizing pattern prior to the assignment of additional responsibilities. Regardless, new responsibilities will be disruptive to that individual because every single request to fulfill those new responsibilities will create further disruption for everyone until that person can develop a self-organizing pattern that works and that can meet the additional challenges. If they are ill-prepared for the challenges, the experience of chaos will be all the more evident to them and to everyone around them.

Two problems come into view for the more vulnerable community members. First, those who are subject to guidance from a socially constructed and therefore inadequate figure of authority are not supported in developing the knowledge or skills they need to maintain their own well-being and to advance their own capacity. Second, accepting guidance from one who lacks a healthy self-organizing pattern compounds rather than assists the resolution of any difficulties. These are not only problems for those under the authority, they are huge problems for the conferee of authority, unless they are well supported by those who appointed them. Status gain won't go far in terms of life satisfaction unless capacity can be developed quickly enough to prevent the loss of reputation and trust. Furthermore, the social mandate to be respectful to a figure of authority is difficult to muster when that authority is unable to fulfill those role requirements.

However, the mandate to respect authority is firmly entrenched in some people. At one point in my occupational therapy career, I was asked to recommend appropriate assistive technology for a child with a disability. In the course of the consultation, we explored what the child could and could not do in terms of reading and writing. A teacher's aide took a lead role in the process and, I noticed, instructed the child to spell her name differently than it was spelled in the information I had been given. I could see no reason for this deviation other than personal preference, so I asked the child's mother why this was being done. She replied that she was taught to respect those who were in a position of authority. Apparently, she believed that being employed by the school was evidence of greater authority than she had as a parent. This illustrates the problematic nature of buying into authority that is conferred for social reasons rather than capacity: it is harmful to those most vulnerable.

Perhaps that aide was not clear about the boundaries of her role. Perhaps she was misinformed about her role. Perhaps she was given more responsibility in other areas of student care and made the assumption that these responsibilities indicated license to teach whatever she wanted. Perhaps she wished to carry a role with more responsibility and was in denial of her feelings about being in the role of a teacher's aide. Couple any of these possibilities with a desire to make the world a better place (read: consistent with her own views of what should be) and a personal preference for a different spelling of the child's name, and voilà! we have a recipe for a problem.

Every player on that child's team, from the aide to the parent to the teacher to the school administrator, participated to some extent in the wrongdoing until it was corrected. It is easy to see how this can happen, because every player may have had a pattern of behavior that did not allow the child's spelling of her own name to be identified as an issue (until my consultation raised the concern). Fortunately, once the problem was brought to light, appropriate steps were taken by figures of authority who were able to meet the challenge in a way that better supported the child's learning and identity development.

Healthcare Relationships

Another arena where people often donate power to an authority figure is in health care. It is true that completion of a degree and license to practice suggests competency—the capacity to use the information that has been learned in the degree process. However, there is a socially constructed aspect in health care provider-patient relationships and a developmental process that makes these relationships complex and sometimes confusing. In occupational therapy practice, relations between an occupational therapist and client can shift over time as both individuals evolve in their understanding of the presenting problem and of one another.[16]

Initially, similar to the approach physicians who practice conventional medicine typically take, an occupational therapist may take a more authoritative approach, acting as an expert and suggesting a plan of action the client might follow. However, therapists may either begin with or move into a relationship that includes discussion and inclusion of the client's beliefs and ideas so that a partnership is established in which there is more equal representation in decisions. Later in an evolving relationship, a client-centered approach could entail the client taking the lead role in how their therapeutic process plays out. In the client-centered approach, the self-organizing pattern is fully enabled so they can move forward and away from health-care services as they develop their capacity for self-care.

Each of these approaches may be used intentionally and independently from the others, but there is often a process of unfolding from therapist-as-expert to client-as-expert. In occupational therapy, what constitutes a therapeutic session can shift dramatically over time as the client's capacity improves.[17] Each session is tailored to pose a just-right challenge that is doable even as it presses the client to develop greater capacity. As challenges are met, new needs become apparent and plans can be made to meet those new challenges—again, via tailored activities that pose only the next just-right challenge. In order to construct the just-right challenge, good communication between occupational therapist and client is required.

This opens the door for shifting decision-making responsibility from the therapist to the client. The collaboration in planning and implementation creates the possibility of flexibility and creativity in the relationship.

Client-centered care, also known as person-centered care, actually originated with Carl Rogers in his counseling practice. He explained his ideas in *The Counseling Psychologist* article "Empathic: An Unappreciated Way of Being." Rogers was aiming for a more humanistic approach than was previously conceptualized in psychotherapeutic theory and practice. Although he fought a tide of misunderstanding about his work, it is now considered one of the most important contributions in the twentieth century. Many other health-related services now ascribe to client-centered therapy. Still, there are always challenges having to do with the figures of authority in health care.

Just the idea of a hierarchical relationship in health care is awkward. Our conceptual model for well-being suggests individuals need to be in charge of their lives, yet we've constructed a health-care system that places people with specific kinds of education in charge of those seeking better health. If that is not confusing enough, there is also some dissonance in what kind of role a health-care practitioner should take in a health-care relationship. For one thing healing practices are based in scientific thinking, and, at least in terms of professional training as a psychotherapist, that presents a problem because the psychotherapy profession is moving toward more use of protocols and techniques to designed to 'fix' a client and this is consistent with patterns of codependency. Therapists who become more healthy have difficulty functioning in a system designed to support codependency.[18]

In my experience practicing occupational therapy, the same dilemma has intruded into my illusions of what a good therapeutic relationship is. On occasion, it became evident that my clients were also confused by this. More than once I have had to clarify whether my primary intent was to keep myself emotionally removed from my client and thus more fully objective, or to connect with care and concern. The role I tended to choose—as a participant rather than objective observer—was not always easy. At times it required that I sit with my client's pain or vulnerability. I had to do this without being thrown off balance because the client was relying on me for stability in their most fragile moments. This is not the kind of capacity that can be taught in the classroom, so the authority that is based on classroom learning cannot adequately respond to every health-care need.

To prepare to meet the bigger challenges in health care, there must also be another kind of preparation. As it currently stands in our health-care practices, the authority based on academic knowledge is coupled with the socially constructed authority idea that new graduates will mature into greater capacity. A significant part of that greater capacity is a strong self-organizing pattern—individuals who know who they are, what they are capable of, and who rest confidently in this knowledge in the face of whatever trauma those around them are experiencing. In the best of all worlds, that greater capacity can also be informed by current and accurate research about what works and what doesn't, and with an understanding that vulnerable individuals do not all sit at the peak of the research bell curve.

In contrast to Western culture health-care practices, Indigenous healing practices are client-centered from beginning to end. Richard Katz points out that whereas Rogers includes listening as an ingredient in good counseling, listening is intrinsic to Indigenous healing. Furthermore, Indigenous healers bring their own wealth of experience to those seeking healing. To do so, they must be balanced themselves.[19] It is easy to make the shift to our conceptual model language. Humility and respect are necessary qualities that come with experience, and with a self-organizing ability to speak and listen with clarity and compassion. Indigenous models of healing, at least in this brief glance, appear to easily align with qualities that support life. They are focused on *healing* rather than curing, which means wholeness and connectedness is what comes into sight rather than removal of symptoms.[20]

When symptoms are treated as experiences in which we can learn about ourselves, the idea of removing them falls quickly into the category of not desirable. Healing that comes from being heard and recognized, on the other hand, allows us an option of more meaning that stretches among physical, emotional, mental, and spiritual dimensions. As we discuss further in chapter 4, this focus aids in adaptation and transformation, such as described by Richard Katz.[21]

There is a blessing and a problem in Western health-care in that many who gravitate toward these professions want to help others. Schaef gets straight to the point. She saw that in many ways, a health-care relationship carries the same qualities as an addictive relationship and concluded that her own struggles with the practitioner-client relationship had characteristics of codependency because our health-care system is designed to make it so.[22] Such a radical and broad-reaching statement needs careful consideration.

For one thing, the very same qualities instilled in psychotherapists exist in, and in fact characterize, those with addictions. For example, psychotherapists are assumed to know what is best for their clients—thus steering discussion away from the possibility that a client might be or might need to be self-organizing. For another thing, psychotherapists limit the conveyance of information (their own perceptions and theories about what is going on with the client) to what they *think* the client can handle. This is potentially a lie of omission. Added to that is the idea that the therapist knows more about their clients than what they know about themselves—another untruth that can confuse the clients' healing process. It is fairly easy to arrive at the conclusion that this imbalance might create dependency of the client on the psychotherapist.[23]

At the same time, the therapist's responsibility to help the client toward health and independence presents a conflict of interest, because once services are no longer needed, the exchange of money also ceases. This raises the possibility that psychotherapists can become financially, if not emotionally, dependent on their clients. Their role as expert lifts them up to a social and financial status they would not otherwise enjoy. We count on ethics to mitigate this problem, and perhaps it does in most cases.

While Schaef acknowledges she may have helped some individuals in her practice of psychotherapy, she also notes the potential for harming those who have come for help. Her "living in process" approach, which evolved from looking closely at *how* she herself was participating, is based on principles of brutal honesty couched in the twelve-step process. Similar to my discussion above about self-knowledge, honesty with oneself and others is a well-known key to addiction recovery. When Schaef realized the psychotherapy profession is ensconced in codependent processes, including dishonesty, she chose to increase her honesty with herself and others by embracing a view of herself as a recovering psychotherapist. Her thoughts about this are articulated in *Beyond Therapy, Beyond Science: A New Model for Healing the Whole Person*. Although Schaef's view and treatment of herself as a recovering psychotherapist may not be viable for many psychotherapists and health-care practitioners, the level of integrity involved in taking that degree of personal responsibility for her own and her clients' welfare evokes respect. Her move to identify as a recovering psychotherapist sets a high standard, not just for other psychotherapists and health-care practitioners but for everyone who enjoys the privilege of socially constructed authority.

Racialization and Socially Constructed Authority

Race is a socially constructed concept that assumes that White people are better than or more capable than Black, Indigenous, or other people of color, and with that comes an assumption that the White person should sit in a position of authority. A White person or the one with lighter skin is always given the position of power.[24] Indeed, as Kendi explains in his *Stamped from the Beginning* book, for the last five hundred years, White people have not only presumed authority over people of color but have codified that authority in many instances of law and public policy, convinced that we are doing Black, Indigenous, or other people of color a favor by getting them to do our work for us. White people are the progeny of plantation bosses, factory bosses, ranking military officers, and homemakers who hire "help," and we have continued to assume authority even, or perhaps especially, when we are incapable of doing the work we want done. This pattern is not self-organizing. It is other-organizing, and puts everyone at risk. The lie about our (White) competence and our (White) disregard for the need others have for self-agency brings the perpetration of harm to a community level, with one entire population perpetrating harm on another. These lies are not so different from the lies an addict tells to avoid facing their addiction.

The constant push to maintain control over the lives of people who are not of European-descent exemplifies, at community and cultural levels, the same dynamic that we saw in figure 2.2, where one person (in this case one population) attempts to control another (population) through manipulation or coercion. Because of the socially constructed hierarchy, there are even more damaging effects. In her work to dismantle White Supremacy, Sharon "Star" Smith (Saponi/Mohawk) speaks of a need by those in power to control the resources (the addict's supply), the narrative (the addict's perspective that their own needs eclipse the needs of others), and the processes (insistence on certain ways of being and doing, and certain degrees of belonging and evolving into greater capacity).

There are similarities between addictive patterns and racism. With the help of two Black friends, Schaef came to understand that White people, including herself, *are* the system of oppression even if compliance with racist ideas and behaviors is unintentional or beyond the scope of awareness. Her conclusion was that unless she was willing to discover and change the unconscious ways she was participating in the system, she would continue to cause harm to herself and others.[25] In short, she met the challenge by learning more about herself and found new and healthier ways to maintain her self-organizing pattern. She sets an excellent example.

When we are young, we develop an understanding of our identity as a family member according to how our family fits into our larger community. We eventually come to identify ourselves according to our region or state of origin or residence, or according to our profession or hobby. But rarely do White people reflect on the history or implications of our White identity. On the other hand, I understand that Black, Indigenous, and other people of color not only are forced to think about their identity every single day, but their skin color informs decisions about what they will say or do on a daily basis.

As we have seen, an increase in self-knowledge can enhance our ability to maintain a self-organizing pattern. It might also help us to be good role models for those who look to us and could improve our relationships with those who are not White. As we will see in the upcoming chapter, our relationships, both peer and hierarchical, are the primary context within which we learn about the world around us and about ourselves.

Key Points

- Transactions with others allow us to nourish and be nourished but require boundaries if those transactions are to be healthy.
- Failure to maintain a self-organizing pattern and good boundaries makes us a liability to ourselves and those around us.
- Disrupted patterns in another are not something we can fix, and trying to do so can create harm for everyone concerned.
- Good boundaries include expressing oneself based on self-knowledge and refraining from making assumptions about the identity and capacity of another individual.
- Figures of authority, whether authentic or socially constructed, have a geometrical advantage in power over those in their care and therefore carry the majority of the responsibility for a healthy

relationship. Listening to those who are more vulnerable is key to carrying that responsibility.

- All forms of oppression, including racialization, domestic and child abuse, class, gender, or disability discrimination, and other injustices can be traced to a poorly constructed self-organizing pattern in the oppressor.

3 PROCESS OF COGNITION

Every time we gain knowledge about ourselves or the world, every skill we add to our repertoire, every time we must reorganize how we think about our troubles and blessings, we become more capable of meeting new, more challenging problems. That is the rosy side of the picture. The process itself, however, can be one of disruption, frustration, and at times despair, depending on how long it takes to integrate a new experience. Sometimes integration is a mere blink, a moment of reflection, and we can move on. Other times it takes longer, sometimes weeks or months or even years, to include a life event into our understanding of who we are. Our pattern of organization, sense of stability, and identity may all be simultaneously disrupted as we incorporate some kinds of new experiences.

Obviously, events that carry more meaning or that disrupt our lives more severely, such as debilitating injuries or serious illnesses, require more time for adjustments. There are so many implications when we unexpectedly lose a beloved family member or the use of a body part. It takes time to develop new resources and new ways of doing things when what we have relied upon is suddenly gone.

Similarly, when events occur in rapid sequence, more time is required to incorporate their meaning into our thinking. A structure that can keep us safe, as well as withstanding these disruptive events, is essential. We will learn more about our dissipative structure in the next chapter, but the process of cognition—how we learn—contributes significantly to such a structure so we will explore that first.

Our previous experiences can be described as a pattern of knowledge that is somewhat stable and organized. A new experience changes that pattern by adding to it without destroying the overall identity expressed.[1] In other words, we process new experiences by determining how they relate to experiences we had in the past, fitting the new information into the pattern of how we view ourselves and the world. When we do this, those new experiences can provide new insights that will help us navigate future challenges. When they are assimilated and organized in our minds, our experiences make us more capable people. We actually recreate who we are as we make these adaptations.[2] And we do so from infancy forward, as long as we live in a way that supports ongoing life.

According to the Piagetian model, human development begins with a focus on sensorimotor experience, attended by social support and emotions regarding what is comfortable or unpleasant. As we gain motor control, we are able to engage more consciously in social encounters, which then become the focus of our learning. Motor skill development does not stop, however. It takes on a supporting role for social skill development, which soon takes on a supporting role as we learn the emotional control necessary to assert our independence and develop meaningful relations. In this way, the Piagetian child-development model suggests a rolling focus across different aspects or dimensions of experience, all intertwined and simultaneously relevant, yet in a clear progression from one dimensional focus to another.[3] Because our very life depends on our ability to continue expanding our capacity, it might be useful to understand how we can keep learning as we age beyond our childhood years.

Accommodating New Information

Let's look first at the mechanics of accommodating new information into our existing pattern of experiences. Figure 3.1 gives us a visual image of the existing pattern and possibilities for introducing new information.

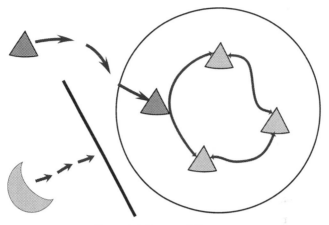

Figure 3.1. Process of Cognition.

In this figure, the triangle outside the circle has a familiar quality because it is similar to the triangles already incorporated into the pattern, although it is a darker shade. Because it is recognizable, it is met with receptivity and can be easily assimilated. A diamond shape could also be incorporated with relative ease because of its similarity to the triangles. However, a stimulus that has no similarity whatsoever with the existing pattern, such as the moon shape, is not so easily incorporated as useful information. It may not even register consciously as something that warrants attention.

Consider a young child in a room full of adults talking about politics. The discussion will probably mean little or nothing to the child, who does not yet have the kinds of experience that would support understanding that discussion. The child will focus on playing, and the voices will be tuned out. However, if the conversation turns to a topic the child can relate to, such as a pet or friend, the child will pay attention and might participate. We might say that in the latter case there is a resonance between the child and the topic being discussed. That resonance opens a door, so to speak, so that the information can be assimilated into the experience of the child and the child's way of thinking.

In order to perceive anything, there must be something already within our experience with which it can resonate.[4] This begs the question of how we can ever learn anything new. One answer is that we build on what we know. If we frequently receive packages of a consistent size and shape in our mail, and these packages bring to us something useful, we will be more likely to open a similar package from an unknown source, perhaps without even realizing it is from a different source. We have an openness to the package because of its familiarity even though this one may contain something we don't need or that is harmful. Our trust in the shape and size of the package is enough to allow further investigation.

Trust, as it turns out, is key to learning because the presence of fear shifts our attention to our survival, raises our defenses, and makes it difficult to focus on anything but our safety. Without some trust to allow receptivity to new experiences, we would likely miss out on valuable information. What if the package we receive is a different size and shape but comes from an individual we trust? Instead of not noticing the difference or wondering about our safety, we would probably be eager to open this package that obviously contains something new and different. Furthermore, we know self-trust underlies trust in others, and approaching something new with a sense of who we are and what our capacity is goes a long way toward being receptive to new information.

Another possible answer to how we can learn what is new is that although a stimulus might not register consciously, it could register in our unconscious mind. For example, unthinkable traumatic events that cannot be assimilated certainly leave a mark on the survivor, though they are often buried in the subconscious. Such an experience also confers a certain kind of knowing, a glimpse of something terrible. Even though this kind of learning is unconscious, it can serve as a point of resonance for future experiences that have similar characteristics.

Different Kinds of Knowing

This brings us to the idea of different kinds of knowing. It is common knowledge that there are five senses upon which we base what we know about the world—we taste, touch, hear, see, and smell. What is not so commonly known is that there are many other senses also present in our biological makeup. For example, our inner ear holds the semicircular canals of the vestibular system, which tells us if we are moving and in what direction, as well as if our head is upside down in relation to earth's gravity. Our muscles and joints are threaded with proprioceptive and kinesthetic sensory neurons that tell us the position of our body parts in relation to one another and the direction and force of the movements of our body parts. I'll be more specific. We can tell, even if we are blind, that our arm is reaching and in what direction. We can also feel, through sensory neurons, vibration, temperature, pressure, and pain. All twelve of these senses, the commonly known five and seven others, are available through our biological body.

Ann Manser suggests there are different planes of experience and receptivity in our being,[5] Her use of the word planes can be considered the same as my use of the word dimensions. She notes, for example, that we hear with our physical ears, but some people demonstrate clairaudience, or the ability to hear something at a distance beyond the range of physical hearing. Others are able to "read" unspoken thoughts, to comprehend the unspoken motives of another, or to hear the admonitions or directives of a spirit-voice not associated with any particular person but which is felt or interpreted as a more universally relevant voice.[6]

For each of the five senses there are nine planes of reception, ranging from physical sensations to spiritual knowing and all degrees of subtlety in between.[7] Although Manser was not aware of other biologically based senses, I and my colleague Sandy Stevens were able to identify a similar range of possible perceptions for the other senses we knew about from our studies of neurobiology and occupational therapy. There is not space enough here to dedicate to a full exploration of the twelve senses and twelve dimensions that emerged from our extrapolations, but identifying some of what Manser, and I and Stevens generated will help our discussion about the process of cognition.

Some of Manser's descriptions[8] suggest activity rather than passive reception, and indeed, the proprioceptive and kinesthetic senses that tell us what our muscles and joints are doing also suggest activity. This is how we learn: by participating so that we are informed by the world even as we contribute what we have to offer. In Piagetian terms, sensorimotor is one word and sensorimotor experience underlies all intelligence. Sensation and action are so closely linked as to be symbiotic. When action occurs, there is sensation whether we are aware of it or not, and when sensation occurs, there is always potential for, if not realized, action.[9]

I have suggested several times now that through our lifetime we experience many different dimensions of experience. I have also suggested that to learn something new, there must be a certain degree of receptivity. Most of us experience many of these receptive phenomena without blinking an eye. We discern, we find our center when we are thrown off balance, we resist, we incubate desire, we navigate increasing awareness, and much more. The sense of responsibility is part of life, as is the sense of flow when we are open to it, and as is the awareness of potential. These common and well-known perceptions provide us with a receptive doorway to learning. However, it is helpful to provide a framework so that we have a way to begin organizing our thoughts about all this lest we become confused or overwhelmed.

More about Accommodating New Information

Let's go back to our circle and triangles for a moment to see what adding a new dimension would look like in those terms. Consider figure 3.2. At the left we see a circle similar to the one on figure 3.1, though this diamond shape has been allowed into consciousness because it is similar to the triangle. The diamond may represent noticing something for the first time, though it has been there all along. Perhaps a child discovers a door not noticed before, though they have been in their grandparents' home many times. Opening that door opens a whole new world for the child: new-to-them objects to explore, to play with, to think about, and perhaps to put to use in the child's own life.

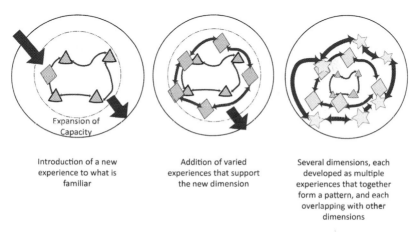

| Introduction of a new experience to what is familiar | Addition of varied experiences that support the new dimension | Several dimensions, each developed as multiple experiences that together form a pattern, and each overlapping with other dimensions |

Figure 3.2. Adding Dimensions of Capacity.

As adults, we don't encounter many new attic doors, but our familiar contexts can provide surprising possibilities that we too can explore, play with, think about, and perhaps put to use in our lives. Consider a conversation you may have with a friend (a familiar triangle event) that turns to discussion of a dream that turned out to be accurately precognitive. Like the attic door, this is intriguing. You decide to pay more attention to your own dreams and read about dream interpretation. By chance, you overhear another friend talking about a dream study group, something you would not have paid any attention to before, but now there is resonance for you and your ears perk up. You ask to join the group, and your experience with dreams is expanded by yet another kind of experience with more possibilities for developing your understanding.

Your first intrigue in your friend's sharing can be seen as that initial diamond shape, and new accumulated information and experiences add capacity to your repertoire, as represented by the additional diamond shapes in the center circle of figure 3.2. You may find that some dreams are in color and others are not, that some seem complicated while others are simply an impression of you sitting and talking with someone. Certain people or animals or pets might show up frequently, causing you to wonder about what those images mean. As you begin to organize your dreams in your mind and observe how they speak to you, that experiential content will become available as a resource to draw upon when you encounter challenges in your daily life. In this way, a new dimension of experience comes into being. But that is not the end of it. You can continue adding to that dimension for the rest of your life.

In order to better understand your dreams, you may find yourself thinking about your ideals due to the symbolic content of your dreams. As you develop this new area of exploration, a whole new dimension will emerge, complete with new perspectives and content that can and will inform you in your dream interpretation and in your waking life. The circle at the right in figure 3.2 shows several dimensions, depicted as diamonds, pentagons, and stars, that connect where the meaning in one dimension overlaps with the meaning in another dimension in the context of a shared experience. We will look at this phenomenon in more detail in chapters 4 and 5, but first let's look at some of the more common dimensions of human experience.

Some authors who write about dimensions of human experience cut the pie in fewer pieces, and some cut it into more. In his *Synthesis of Yoga*, Sri Aurobindo writes about humans developing toward a state of perfection characterized by an experience of wholeness. More specifically, he discusses three bodies: the gross body (food sheath and vital vehicle), the subtle body (mental vehicle), and the causal body (knowledge and bliss).[10] Manser writes about twelve states of consciousness or planes of experience ranging in degrees of subtlety from the physical (similar to

Aurobindo's gross body) to the spiritual (similar to Aurobindo's causal body of knowledge and bliss).[11] Piaget and Inhelder, in *Psychology of the Child,* write about several domains of development that unfold during childhood years. Stanislav Grof writes about four types of psychedelic experience and the relevance of these to human health and well-being.[12]

I draw my ideas from all these scholars and also include ideas from various writings of Carl Jung because Manser and Grof reference his work. Rather than attempting to delineate all possible ways to cut the human experience pie, however, what I offer is a compilation of ideas about human experience in eight dimensions and in terms of our process of cognition.

Dimensions

A common way to use the word dimension is in terms of one dimensional versus two-dimensional versus three-dimensional versus four-dimensional. In this usage, the single dimension is a single point. The two-dimensional object is a single point extended into a line. A three-dimensional object has lines that go in three directions, so there is now volume created by depth. A fourth dimension frequently refers to the addition of time. The first identified dimension has a direct relationship with the second because a line is an extension of a single point. Similarly, the depth in a three-dimensional object has a relationship with and extends the encompassed two-dimensional planes. Time expands an object with depth to include the possibility of change.

Whereas Piaget and his colleagues refer to developmental stages of intelligence[13], Grof refers to four types of experience[14], Manser writes about planes of consciousness,[15] and other scholars use other terms. I use the word dimension because it reminds me that there are facets of life experience that are unique yet seem to have encompassing or encompassed relationships with other facets. I also note that our typical usage of the term dimension reflects increasing capacity and complexity as the numbers go up. Similarly, developing capacity in different dimensions of human experience adds complexity at every juncture. And as with the fourth dimension of time, I see dimensions of human experience appearing to increase in subtlety as we shift our focus from the physical toward spiritual experience.

I decline the urge to describe the full development of each dimension here. Instead, I provide a basic definition according to my interpretation, a glimpse of the anchors for each dimension as they appear prior to the rise of focus on that dimension, the kinds of outer experience (how we occupy ourselves) and inner experience (receptivity) relevant to each, and the problems that cannot be solved within the dimension itself and thus require development of other new capacities.

The sequence offered here is how I see the spectrum expanding from tangible physical experiences to universal and often elusive subtle experiences. Although I lay this out in linear form, the line is not necessarily straight, nor do we learn everything in one dimension before moving on to another. We might say that our development occurs in a spiral fashion as we loop back to refine motor or social or other skills when new situations require more refined or expanded capacity.

There is also a need to consider whether our development is focused on knowing more about the external world or on learning about ourselves. In figure 3.3, the development of new dimensions is reflected in increasingly larger circles that encompass the smaller, previously developed dimensions. The figure also shows how development of dimensions shifts between an outer and inner focus. Circles that sit upward of the horizontal line represent dimensions that are more focused on learning about the external world, and the circles that drop below the line represent dimensions relevant to the expansion of self-knowledge. The fact that overall expansion appears to alternate between the inner and outer worlds speaks to our need for engagement with the world to learn about ourselves and our need to deepen into ourselves in order to address the challenges of participating in the outer world.

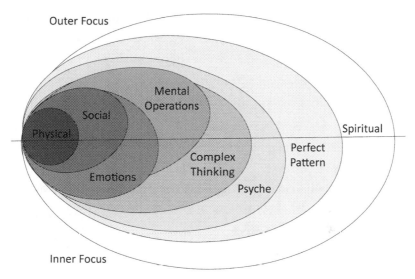

Outer Focus

Mental Operations

Social

Physical

Spiritual

Complex Thinking

Perfect Pattern

Emotions

Psyche

Inner Focus

Figure 3.3. Focus on Inner–World or Outer-World Experiences.

Descriptions of Eight Dimensions

1. Physical

The physical dimension refers to the experience of embodiment, including sensorimotor experience, and the function of all bodily organs and organ systems. The fact that sensation and movement are always in relation to one another and are equally represented demonstrates the remarkable integration between our inner and outer experiences.

Anchor: Genetics and nurturance inform our physical experience.

Outer-world experience: We act in response to what we feel. Although newborn infants are not capable of intentional or coordinated movement, these and more capacities develop quickly as the outer world calls us to participate in exploration and mastery efforts. Self-care, crafts, homemaking, gardening, writing and drawing, and sports are just a few of the many outer-world experiences that can enhance physical capacity into adult and aging years.

Inner-world experience: Maturation of sensorimotor capacity creates a sense of trust in oneself. Early childhood perceptions inform an inner map of oneself, an understanding of the body's size, shape, and capacities. There are twelve biological sensations: auditory, gustatory, kinesthesia, olfactory, pain, pressure, proprioception, temperature, touch, vestibular, vibration, and vision, which mature into refined perceptibility during childhood years. Also in early years is awareness of bodily comfort and discomfort. In later years, awareness, interpretation, and care of other bodily systems, such as digestive, cardiorespiratory, immune, elimination, and nervous systems can also be refined, as can awareness of changes in organ function and energy levels.

Problems not solvable within this dimension: Infants and young children with basic sensorimotor skills cannot yet care for themselves. They need caregivers. Even with more developed physical skills, interaction and support from others is necessary for our acquisition of food, shelter, and safety, as well as a sense of belonging.

2. **Social**

The social dimension refers to the development of capacity to engage in relationships with other people during direct contact and with regard to cultural understanding. When developmental focus shifts to this dimension, it shifts outward in order to learn what is expected and what consequences follow certain behaviors or words. In figure 3.3 the social dimension is shown encompassing the physical dimension and with more experiential content in the outer world than in the inner world.

Anchors: Caregiver-infant transactions provide the basis for our social experiences throughout life. Attachment to a trustworthy caregiver is at the heart of development of self-trust and trust of others, and these trusts are foundational to the social dimension.

Outer-world experience: Ways of interacting and behavior regulation develop first within the family and then within an expanding circle of extended family and friends. Interactions in different environments such as home, daycare, school, faith groups, and other community settings add nuanced skills depending on what is required in each setting. Playing various roles and taking on responsibility according to those roles, including decision-making for social events, economics, political participation, health care, and education, adds capacity. Specific social skills that can be developed include leadership, nurturing, relationship maintenance, organizing, witnessing, and providing information, among others.

Inner-world experience: A sense of identity is constant, although some aspects shift as new experiences add new perspectives about that identity. These changes create fluctuations in one's ability to communicate with others, which may add a sense of frustration, satisfaction, or other emotions to inner experience. A sense of belonging also shifts according to the fluctuations in communication. Caring about others, loving others, and feeling cared for and loved are inner experiences that make participation in outer-world events more feasible.

Problems not solvable within this dimension: It is sometimes difficult to know with whom should we spend more time and what outer-world activities we should engage in.

3. Emotional Dimension

The emotional dimension refers to experiences spanning the full spectrum of emotions including all variations of joy, anger, sorrow, fear, and the desire to fulfill one's needs. Implicit in emotional development is learning to sit with any emotion in the spectrum without harming oneself or others. Figure 3.3 shows the emotional dimension as being primarily an inner experience and as encompassing the social and physical dimensions.

Anchors: Feelings based on sensations of comfort or discomfort arise during sensorimotor experiences and as a result of how others respond to our words and actions.

Outer-world experience: Emotions are always inner-world events. However, our transactions with the outer world give rise to different feelings, and we observe how others express their feelings, so outer-world events are relevant to the development of our emotional dimension. How we express our feelings impacts our subsequent experience as well as the experience of others. One aspect of development of the emotional dimension is discernment about what to share, and where, and when.

Inner-world experience: Different feelings wash over us like a wave washes over sand. More than a hundred words in the English language represent different emotions. Most are nuances of a short set that includes sadness, anger, joy, and fear. The capacity to allow any of these that arises, to allow it to wash over us and then drift away frees us to participate fully in life events. Feelings help us to decide where and when we will engage. They are tied to desire (or not), which is at the root of our impetus to live and to feel alive, to impact those around us and be impacted by them, to activate ideas and navigate challenges. We engage in what is motivating to us and in what we find interesting. As we mature, desire (motivation or interest) can include feelings of responsibility first to oneself and then for others. Empathy and compassion can also be considered relevant in the emotional dimension because both suggest an inner capacity to feel what others feel.

Problems not solvable within this dimension: Although emotions steer us toward or away from certain people or events, they don't give us all the information we need. Some charismatic people whom we think we want to spend time with may prove to be harmful or uninteresting when we get a closer look. Mixed emotions about whether or how or when to participate in what life puts in front of us sometimes leave us hanging, unable to choose.

4. **Mental Operations**

The dimension of mental operations expands our capacity to include an understanding of and ability to act upon the world. We add and subtract, categorize and classify, sequence, manage our space and time, and adjust the speed with which we proceed. The mental operations dimension of experience is primarily above the line in figure 3.3 because we are literally learning about the outer world. Even our inner knowing in this dimension takes cues from what others know and from what is collectively determined to be objective knowledge.

Anchors: Sensorimotor experiences, particularly the vestibular (orientation in space), proprioceptive and kinesthetic (movement of one body part in relation to another body part), and touch are anchors for our mental operations processes because they provide us with dependable information about our position during our interactions with the outer world. Reliable role models in early years provide the emotional arm of this anchor. In both sensorimotor and emotional development, consistency gives us the basis for understanding facts as trustworthy information upon which we can build other knowledge.

Outer-world experience: We build mental operations capacity by assimilating the facts given to us by trustworthy role models and through exploration of our environment. Western culture provides many areas of knowledge with which we can populate our mental operations experience. We learn math and reading skills, and scientific facts, especially from Newtonian and Cartesian perspectives. We might also learn about nutrition or human anatomy and physiology. The more subjects we study, and the more mental operations in which we become proficient, the more fluent will be our use of the mental operations dimension.

Specific to sustaining life, the more we know about how our bodies function, the better prepared we will be to take care of ourselves and to partner with our health-care practitioners. The more we know about different kinds of health care, the better prepared we will be to select a health-care path that will meet our needs. The more we know about how to feed, clothe, and house ourselves in a way that maintains our resources, the better prepared we will be to live in peace with ourselves and others.

And the more we know about other cultures, the better prepared we will be to find community regardless of where we are.

Inner-world experience: We are aware of changes in the environment and in our bodies as we participate in life events. Beyond the emotional pull, we have thoughts about how, how much, when, and where we will participate in available events. We may be interested in an activity, or not. We may feel a hunger for more information, or we may be overwhelmed by the circumstances we face. Manser suggests that our ability to discern direction occurs in this dimension.[16] We also think about or discern a way to sort the facts of a situation in order to find a logical way forward. Our awareness of the environment and of other people includes an awareness of suffering.

Problems not solvable within this dimension: Lived experience is neither simple nor straightforward. For example, being aware of our bodies may raise questions about why we are prone to certain health-related experiences, and this may be more complex than a set of facts. The relations among contributing factors becomes important.

5. **Complex Mental**

The complex mental dimension is all about the ability to think abstractly, to conceptualize, to see patterns, and to add new perspectives to our lived experiences. The relations among various facts and fields of study come into clarity as we expand our thinking beyond the facts and into thinking about patterns and systems. The complex mental dimension also signifies the beginning of self-reflection, and thus the consideration of two points of view (self and other) simultaneously and in relation to one another. In figure 3.3, the complex mental dimension is depicted as returning to a more balanced position between the inner and outer, though still leaning somewhat toward the outer-world experiences.

Anchors: The same anchors that were relevant for the mental operations dimension are relevant here also. Additionally, the knowledge that rests in the mental operations dimension is an anchor for development of the complex mental dimension.

Outer-world experience: Navigating wider communities in our social relations, health care, economic ventures, political action, and education provides us with opportunities to explore how those areas of experience relate to one another. As our dimensions of experience expand and increase in complexity, much more can be said about our outer-world experience. For the sake of brevity, I focus here on the essence of what keeps us alive and well—self-care and health care. Readers can imagine similar descriptors for other areas of experience.

In terms of what sustains life, the complex mental dimension becomes more essential to our process as we age into more rigid patterns of being and doing and more challenges to our health. Self-care requires keeping ourselves in balance—managing workplace or relationship stresses, finding time for ourselves as well as others, and choosing our comrades and health-care practitioners. We occupy ourselves with learning about different facets of ourselves and health-care providers who can help us maintain our ability to function. We also occupy ourselves with scheduling and meeting appointments and navigating insurance agency procedures to file a claim. These activities require an understanding of different organizations and systems.

Although many readers will automatically think about different aspects of health in terms of services, such as eye care, dental care, counseling, cardiac care, and mental health care, among others, there are other kinds of health care that are different from conventional allopathic care that might be useful, if not essential, to our well-being. Alternative and complementary health-care approaches, such as body work (chiropractic care, massage, etc.), Chinese medicine, homeopathy, and Indigenous health-care practices are designed to address the imbalances that underlie diseases from a wholistic perspective. These models are often overlooked because Western culture, with its intense focus on Newtonian-Cartesian thinking, carries a certain amount of bias against knowledge that is centered instead in an understanding of the energetic web that supports all life and the qualities that support that web. In order to choose accurately what will meet our needs, we must navigate different sources of information about health-care philosophies and models of practice.

In the course of meeting our needs, we may interact with people from different walks of life, who identify with different cultural groups and who see the world differently. We have opportunities to collaborate and cooperate with people who have occupations and values and priorities that are different from our own. In order to conduct successful transactions, we learn about the differences and similarities. If we are responsible for others, as we saw in chapter 2, our outer-world experience is more complicated and entails function of the complex mental dimension. In and through all our transactions we experience the consequences of the impact we have on others.

Inner-world experience: Included here is reflection on our roles and contributions, what we've done that worked or didn't, and how we feel about it. We may feel a desire to understand the dynamics of different situations, which means understanding the perspectives of others and opening more to empathy. We juggle ideas about how our experiences fit together, and have ah-ha moments when the dots suddenly connect, or feel a sense of resolution when we discover patterns that suddenly make sense of opposing pieces of information. We may feel motivated to find underlying reasons for certain behavior and events, or to discover, in Manser's words, incentive toward a goal.[17] Other descriptors from Manser's writing about this dimension include comprehension of motives, value of idealism, and awareness of potential for creation.[18]

Examination of the narratives and art expressions of people under the influence of LSD provides unique insight into our inner-world experience.[19] Although LSD sets up a context contrary to natural lived experience, the inner world that is revealed is not inauthentic. Grof is convinced that his discussion about psychedelic types of experience is relevant to states of consciousness that occur, without drugs, in a variety of nonordinary experiences, including experiential psychotherapies, spiritual practices, and near-death experiences, among others. He argues further that because these nonordinary states occur spontaneously, they have validity in any discussion about human well-being.[20] They are justifiably valid examples of lived experience even though they may not occur frequently or in the context of daily habits and routines.

Grof suggests four types of psychedelic experience. He calls the first type abstract or aesthetic, and indeed, it has characteristics that are similar to those of complex thinking which I have just said includes abstraction. Grof's research shows that the experiences of the abstract or aesthetic type can all be explained using Newtonian-Cartesian thinking. They are often visual experiences such as complex geometrical or architectural forms, or auditory experiences such as chimes, buzzing, or chirping. Sensations of touch, smell, or taste might occur, though the latter two are more uncommon. These sensations do not signal an increase in self-knowledge and have no symbolic content that would evoke looking for more meaning.[21] The expanded and complex nature of these experiences suggests relevance in the complex mental dimension rather than in the physical dimension where sensorimotor experiences are directly related to functioning in the tangible world.

Problems not solvable within this dimension: Grof suggests that an abstract psychedelic experience may actually serve as a barrier to further development because such striking sensory experiences can be a distraction from the more difficult path of gaining capacity through exploring our personal and collective history.[22] However, attempts to sort the complex ideas that make up the fabric of our lived experience means we must consider the probability of hidden variables—a term used by David Bohm in his 1952 article that refers to factors that influence lived experience from a place out of sight and not in conscious awareness. With all its patterns and relationships, our complex mental dimension is not prepared to give credence to what is not seen.

6. Psyche

The psyche is already teeming with knowledge and is active in some ways, even before we begin our exploration of this dimension. But that knowledge, sometimes called our shadow, is not yet in our conscious awareness. Development of our psyche dimension occurs as we bring that shadow material into our conscious mind and integrate it into our existing patterns of thinking, feeling, and doing.[23] In figure 3.3 provided earlier in this chapter, the psyche dimension drops back below the horizontal line, marking it as a primarily inner experience. It encompasses every dimension discussed up to this point. It adds complexity and presents itself as more subtle than any dimension thus far.

One reason the psyche appears more complex than previously discussed dimensions is that there can be and probably is significant emotional content in what lies below our level of conscious awareness. In fact, if that content were easy to assimilate, it probably would already be in our conscious awareness. Events such as birth, death, and trauma disrupt whatever patterns were previously in place. This includes new beginnings and endings, such as marriage, divorce, a new career, or a literal or symbolic journey. One reason psyche experiences are more subtle than the complex mental experiences is that whereas complex thinking and complex images have direct ties to outer world and tangible experiences, psyche experiences are elusive. They make waves across our lived experiences as though they have a will of their own and are often difficult to place into a pattern that makes sense.

Anchors: Unexplainable experiences across our lifetime anchor the possibility of hidden variables as influences in our lives. For example, many people experience a rise of strong emotions in situations that don't seem to call for such intensity. A desire for greater understanding of those unexplained events provides the drive needed to explore and develop the psyche. Experiences of playing creatively or using one's imagination provide a base of capacity for exploring this unknown territory.

Outer-world experience: Although the psyche is primarily an inner-world terrain, there are many possible approaches to developing the psyche that entail occupying oneself in outer-world experiences. Development of the psyche is advanced through active dream work which may entail keeping a journal. It is also advanced through the use of symbols or metaphor in creative efforts such as painting, drawing, working with clay, wood, or fiber (e.g., sewing, weaving, knitting). We use our imagination in our recreational occupations, in how we dress, and how we decorate the spaces we reside within. We engage with different people and thus discover where our emotional triggers lie.

Any or all of these occupations have potential to help us slip beyond Grof's sensory barrier[24] and the barrier imposed by a need to hold on to what is already known. These occupations require and build endurance just as our physical body builds strength through use, but only if we participate with an intention to slip beyond those barriers. Simply dreaming, even remembering dreams, barely scratches the surface. Individuals who analyze their dream content for relevance to their inner and outer experiences, however, can be said to be developing capacity in their psyche dimension. Similarly, engaging in creative projects does little to develop the psyche, but attending to or developing metaphoric content does have potential for advancing the capacity of the psyche. Developing the psyche is difficult work for many people, full of traps to keep us feeling comfortable so a supportive mentor, guide, or counselor may need to be employed. Contacting, connecting, and sustaining such a relationship is part of the outer-world experience that supports development of the psyche.

Inner-world experience: Grof's second type of psychedelic experience is described as psychodynamic, biographical, or recollective because his research participants relived emotional and traumatic events from their early years, including their first days of life. Reliving an event may be accompanied by a narrative that contains new understanding about how subsequent life events and relationships unfolded, as well as containing the entirety of the initial event. That new narrative signifies the integration of the event into the organizational pattern so that the new information can take on qualities of sensibility and accessibility for future use.[25]

Access to the psyche is not easy. Our preoccupation with sensations is only one way we keep ourselves in the dark. Emotionally laden events are tucked away for a reason. We may consciously choose to keep an experience out of sight and out of mind because we lack the time or patience or skill required to incorporate it into our pattern of thinking. But memories may rise up whether we want to look at them or not. Conversely, an individual may want to look at a known or suspected emotional trauma, but find that those memories aren't retrieved quickly or easily.[26] Frustration and despair may characterize our experience and willpower to push through the difficult moments and trust in our process are, in my mind, essential to the process.

Inner experiences of the psyche dimension are similar to the emotional dimension experiences discussed earlier, but they differ in that the degree of self-trust that must be practiced is much greater. There is more at stake here than comfort and discomfort. We are talking about our place in not just our family or social circles, not just in the global community, but our very existence as unique and valuable beings, and with that a deep and abiding sense of belonging.

Problems not solvable within this dimension: Navigating the vast unknowns in our psyche means we are moving along our dimensional spectrum toward ever more subtle and complex bases of experience and self-knowledge. The deep and abiding sense of belonging that becomes possible raises the question of what roles we play in the larger scheme of things, what we are good at doing, and what we are not so good at doing. I'm not talking about learned skills, such as making a cake or doing algebra. I'm talking about what subtle qualities define our identity. The highly subjective nature of the psyche cannot answer this because its focus is too much on inner experience. A different perspective is needed to bring us back into a balance between our inner and outer worlds.

7. Perfect Pattern

Manser uses the term "Perfect Pattern" to describe an archetypal model, a gift from spirit that we humans can use as a guide as we develop our capacity to be fully aware beings.[27] We saw earlier that the self-organizing pattern can be discussed in terms of authentic identity, habits and routines, and expanding capacity as different challenges are faced. Similarly, our Perfect Pattern dimension can be discussed in terms of the values and ideals that inform how we see ourselves and in the roles we assume, as well as in terms of our experiences with the rhythm and balance that guide universal experiences such as birth and death. The Perfect Pattern dimension reflects the same meaning as maintaining a self-organizing pattern, but because of the more universal content, the reflection is more subtle and complex than we have discussed before. Additionally, experience in this dimension offers a merging of polarities, such as birth and death, spirit and tangible, male and female. Figure 3.3 shows the Perfect Pattern dimension as returning to more equal representation of inner and outer experiences after our deep dive into the inner world of the psyche.

Anchors: Maintaining a self-organizing pattern in daily life as we face dissonance and disruptions is preparatory work for embracing and developing our perfect pattern dimension. Our experiences of embracing role models either in person or story form also help to set the stage for developing toward an ideal way of being and doing. Practices such as martial arts, yoga, and music, which are characterized by an integration of mental and physical effort and striving for perfect form, also support the development of the Perfect Pattern dimension.

In figure 3.3, the Perfect Pattern dimension is depicted as nearly balanced between outer and inner experience, which shifts our focus from the dichotomous outer versus inner experiences to a greater sense of wholeness. In the perfect-pattern dimension, that sense of wholeness can be experienced more profoundly than our development of more tangible dimensions because it is not simply a matter of attending to and integrating our outer and inner worlds; we now have all the capacity provided by the psyche, the complex mental dimension, the mental operations, and the emotional and social dimensions to incorporate into our decisions and our ways of being and doing. This means integration of polarities is multifaceted. Let's look at how that occurs, still with consideration of our outer and inner experiences, but now showing more about how the inner supports outer experiences and vice versa.

Outer-world experience: The physical body is necessary to a spiritual life.[28] More specifically, the physical, sensory-laden experiences available to us via worldly transactions are crucial to every stage of spiritual development.[29] This means that how we choose to occupy ourselves—perhaps in a practice of yoga, a commitment to gardening, or the care of a loved one—can facilitate our health while giving us time to make connections with others, ourselves, nature, or a higher power. We design experiences to help us make these life-affirming connections. We participate in rituals with symbolic content or prayer, gather in worship or celebration or grieving, and study ideas we believe are aligned with universal truths, love, or peace. In addition to these occupations driven by an intent to live into our ideals, we can look for archetypes as we go about our other daily routines.[30]

The word archetype means different things to different people.[31] For spiritual seekers, archetypes may arise from the collective unconscious—the terrain in Jungian philosophy that holds the buried collective knowledge of humanity. For those committed to religious beliefs, it may mean different facets of one God, such as the various archangels or the Roman or Greek deities. Some people interpret archetypes to mean controlling paradigms or metaphors. Still others see them as holograms that are both outside and within us.[32]

For people interested in human growth and development, the word guide, or guides, may explain what an archetype is.[33] Neither Native American author of *Animal Speak: The Spiritual & Magical Powers of*

Creatures Great and Small Ted Andrews nor Native American coauthors of *Medicine Cards: The Discovery of Power through the Ways of Animals* Jamie Sams and David Carson use the word archetype, but they do describe a worldview that interprets animals as guides for navigating life and health.

Because each archetype embodies an ideal composite of values that might drive our decisions, they serve as a bridge between the most subtle and most tangible aspects of life. The values we prioritize determine what we pay attention to and how we choose to occupy ourselves. For example, an archetypal mother can be described with a list of qualities such as the ability to nurture, teach, and carry responsibility for a child. Paying attention to these qualities informs our choices as we carry out a mothering role, infusing them ever so subtly with spiritual content. This explains how holding the values of protecting and supporting life, as in Hasselkus' example of caregiving I mentioned in chapter 1, transforms a mundane occupation to a ritual.

In *Awakening the Heroes Within: Twelve Archetypes to Help Us Find Ourselves and Transform Our World,* Pearson lists and describes twelve archetypes. Some appear more desirable, while others are more difficult to embrace, but they are all part of our lives. There are those that espouse nurturing and those that destroy, those that protect and those that play tricks. The specific archetypal content that comes up as we carry out our roles informs our priorities. It is in part determined by our developmental status. Children are more likely to be working with archetypes of the innocent and the orphan. For teens it may be the lover and seeker, and in early adult years caregiver and warrior archetypes tend to come to the fore. The latter is especially relevant for those who engage in advocacy work, legal work, or who work long or hard shifts, as well as for those who sign up for military service.[34]

Although caregiving and being a warrior seem diametrically opposed, values of endurance and resilience are relevant to both. Our life paths may play out in such a way that we seem to take up one or the other of each pair. In reality we probably alternate our focus, attempting to bring each into maturity. In doing so we bring them into balance with one another and develop the values common to both. It is the challenges we face in the roles we play, often inadvertently, that raise our awareness of the values and ideals we seek to embody. Similarly, when Andrew's (*Animal Speak*) or Sams and Carson's (*Medicine Cards*) animals show up repeatedly in someone's life, that animal is considered a totem—a guiding force that teaches via that particular animal's ways of being and doing.

The values expressed by the archetypes or animals don't always show up in a positive way in our lives. For Pearson, with her Jungian orientation, this means that lack of awareness of an archetype's influence is reflected in problematic thoughts and behaviors.[35] For each medicine card description Sams and Carson use the term "contrary" to describe an undesirable influence created by denial or lack of understanding of the gifts given through the presence of the animal. Similarly, for each animal described, Andrews raises specific questions for reflection for when some animal shows up, lest in our ignorance we behave or speak in a way that is offensive to others or to our own sense of well-being.

We looked earlier at how lack of self-knowledge can impair our capacity for clear communication and respectful behavior. Now we see that greater understanding of the different archetypes, no matter which frame we choose to use, can help us understand ourselves more accurately and more thoroughly. Those archetypal figures that show up in our interactions with others and in the natural environment give us clues about who we are and how to proceed with civility and care.

Our relations with archetypes can change over time and as that occurs, our outer-world experiences also change. Once we shine the light on the shadow or contrariness and bring its content into our awareness, our potential for troublesome thoughts and behavior is significantly less, and our potential for developing new capacity grows. Any archetype in shadow form can underlie an addiction that aligns with that specific archetype. Pearson identifies various manifestations of this. For example, the addiction that aligns with the archetype of caregiver might be codependency. For the lover archetype, the addiction could be a need for relationship or sex. For the sage archetype, which typically comes to the fore in the later years of life, Pearson suggests giving up attachments which could apply to any addiction.[36]

The solution to addiction is to grow in self-knowledge by developing our understanding of the archetype as it manifests in us. This approach carries the potential to transform what is problematic into a positive influence. As self-knowledge increases, indeed, as we age, other archetypes may emerge into consciousness with other shadow (and problematic) material. The rhythm and balance in the rise and integration of archetypal content brings us back to the highly charged cyclical themes of birth and death.

In our daily lives we develop habits and routines that reflect our individual values. These are imbedded in the cycles of life and death where the theme of birth may be enacted through actual birth as a human, or through embarkment on a new career, relationship, or other path that is significantly different. In any case, that birth also represents a death to some previous pattern of being and doing. Contrarily, every death, whether the death of a human being or the end of a career or relationship, signals a birth of something new. Such changes, especially when they occur suddenly and without forewarning, can be traumatic, so trauma can be interpreted as a birth/death event. As long as the trauma is left unprocessed, its potential to increase capacity is thwarted—perhaps experienced as hanging in limbo in that birth/death dichotomy. Such a status will cast its shadow over every decision a traumatized individual makes.

Inner-world experience: Grof calls his third type of psychedelic experience a perinatal experience. He found that his LSD participant's experiences of this type build on the psychodynamic, biographical, and recollective psychedelic experience. The perinatal expands recall from the emotional focus of the psychodynamic type of experience to new levels of complexity and subtlety in death and rebirth processes and a far more detailed view of the physical and physiological changes experienced during birth. Fetal position, obstetric interventions, changes in skin color, and sensations of choking, as well as existential content (e.g., the meaning of existence, unity with or separation from the mother) were available for reexperiencing with the greater awareness offered by the influence of LSD.[38] This reflects an increase in complexity from the psychodynamic type of experience. The perinatal experience is more subtle than the psychodynamic type of experience because it brings death and rebirth into focus as universal truths that can only be expressed in symbolic form, and that transcend cultural, racial, and educational backgrounds of individuals.

The idea of death and rebirth is reminiscent of the duality of being pulled simultaneously in two directions (comfort-discomfort). Memories of hellish experiences arrive with a hidden blessing. Blissful infatuation marks the beginning of a fatal love affair. Duality is also apparent in the perinatal psychedelic experience, in terms of death and rebirth. Imagine if, when faced with a situation confused by pulls to approach and pulls to avoid, instead of thinking about the state of confusion itself, we instead were to think in terms of death and birth—not of our human life but of which values we want to promote and which we are ready to discard. This is not an excuse to linger in any role that continues abusive patterns but is a suggestion that the values we choose to embrace can serve as a guide through trauma or a difficult passage, and they perhaps might show us a way out of an abusive relationship. I believe many people do this already, although without attaching the depth of meaning inherent in a death-rebirth conversation.

At the center of these life-death experiential themes is the reality that the two seemingly opposite kinds of experience are so closely linked as to be inseparable. When death occurs, birth of a new way of being and doing arrives every time; and when we experience being born anew, an old pattern is demolished. Navigating these transitions occurs often, if not every day, for everyone. The Perfect Pattern dimension, though, is an even more subtle and complex experience of those events *if* we choose to focus on that rather than on the mundane activities where the details of living and dying play out.

Inner-world experience is characterized by the degree of effort made to develop a relationship with the world around us. These experiences can range from suffering from a belief that we can never get enough of some kind of external support (the quintessential opposite to the self-organizing pattern) or from being at odds with everything and everyone else, to experiences that are rich with meaning in metaphor and symbolism. In *Awakening the Heroes* Pearson describes several levels of maturity for each archetype that reflect the range of experience. Her descriptions of the Shadow level generally include some form of denial. The Call level describes what beckons us to work with the archetype. Levels One, Two, and Three reflect different degrees of engagement and understanding of the archetypal content. For Level Three, the most mature, descriptors include words such as trust and optimism, wisdom, realistic expectations, honesty, increased communication, community building, transformation, radical self-acceptance, living in the moment, knowledge that everything is connected to everything else, and fully utilizing all resources. Manser's descriptors of the two planes just prior to the spiritual plane in their spectrum of dimensions focus on understanding and alignment with the Perfect Pattern and repeated use of the phrase "full comprehension and understanding" of various kinds of sensory-themed information.[39] The integration of dimensions, of time factors, and of seemingly dichotomous pairs appears pleasantly fruitful after the difficult terrain of the psyche.

Problems not solvable within this dimension: Even those who work on integration of each archetypal pair rarely if ever come to a place where all six pairs are fully matured. The vast majority of the human population will see no end to the struggle of developing a permanent sense of balance.[40]

8. Spiritual

The spiritual dimension refers to the relationship one has with a higher power, whether that be framed as a deity, or as All That Is, or as a global or universal ecology. Spiritual capacity may be facilitated through religious practices or commitment to daily occupations that emphasize striving to learn more, following one's heart while listening respectfully to others, relieving one's stress through manifesting one's deeply held values, and occupying oneself with meaningful tasks. Figure 3.3 (posted earlier in this chapter) shows the spiritual dimension returned to the center, balanced equally between inner and outer experiences as was the sensorimotor dimension, but here so much greater in capacity.

Anchors: According to Chopra, all aspects of spiritual development depend on our full embodiment in tangible experiences.[41] This means not only the sensations available across our lived experience, but the emotional content and our struggles to make sense of what seems insensible are also anchors for development of the spiritual dimension.

Outer-world experience: Ritual, worship, meditation, and prayer are practices that support the development of our spiritual dimension. Other activities that build spiritual identity are providing life supporting services to others, engaging respectfully with the natural environment, and creative endeavors. Reflection upon our identity in the larger scheme of things and upon our behavior through a lens of what supports life or spiritual tenets during these outer-world experiences contributes to our spiritual identity.

Inner-world experience: Grof's fourth type of psychedelic experience is identified as transpersonal because these experiences cross the bounds of time and space and ego. Some people who took the LSD regressed to an earlier life in either embryonic form or in a different incarnation, or breached the boundaries between themselves and other people, between themselves and animals, or even between themselves and inanimate objects. In these experiences the integration of the individual with the outer world was such that consciousness was experienced as being at one with all.[42]

The complexity in these kinds of experience is obvious because they transcends space, time, and identity, suggesting so much more in terms of hidden variables that inform us. How spiritual capacity of this transpersonal nature might inform values and ideals is fairly evident. If we are, as psychedelic experiences and some spiritual experiences from other forms of participation suggest, at one with all, then in order to care for ourselves we must also care for all. Indeed, this is a theme in all major spiritual paths and religions. It is also reflected in the self-organizing pattern that mandates respect and honor for the self-agency of others and in the encompassing network layers that are present in all forms of life. Manser's descriptions of sensation for this dimension include full participation in creation and full assimilation of spirit, among others.[43] On the expanded map of Manser's descriptions developed by Stevens and myself, the spiritual dimension includes phrases such as realization of universal balance, full participation with spirit, full comprehension of synchronicity, and brotherly love for all.

Problems not solvable within this dimension: Although such a rosy picture of possible experiences is tantalizing, given the natural shifts in our external world, holding on to this dimension of experience is not possible for the vast majority of individuals. We are rocked by the changes around us, and although a well-developed spiritual dimension can help us to regain our balance quickly in the face of disruption, our balance is disrupted. In fact, it is important that we be disrupted in order to maintain our anchor of embodiment in lived experience, and thus in order to sustain our whole being.

Capacity of Our Whole Self

The sources of meaning in everyday life can be viewed as a continuum that unfolds as we occupy ourselves over time.[44] Applying this idea to the concept of human development, we see that each new dimension is inextricably intertwined with the previously existing pattern through the anchors of experience and in how we occupy ourselves. In Hasselkus' words, "Each instance of authentic experiencing in our daily lives demands anew from us consideration of what is possible for us. We are always balancing the actual with the possible."[45] In other words, how we occupy ourselves opens us to new capacity and understandings. What we do may be focused in one or another dimension, but that experience will open us up to new perspectives. Thus through our occupations each dimension of experience supports the development of dimensions still dormant and all dimensions are intertwined whether they are developed or not.

Though it is possible to be focused primarily in one dimension, we are not usually limited in that way. Even when we engage in a primarily intellectual activity, an office job for example, we hold a physical presence within a social context where we interact using the social skills we learned when we were young such as greeting one another, sharing, appreciating, and helping. Our emotions may be triggered, but we can think through those; and we use our minds to plan, execute our jobs, and keep in perspective how our work fits into the larger picture of society and how our uniqueness is revealed through what we do and how we do it. We may have fears or dreams related to our work situation, and we hold ideals about the best way to participate and perform. If we are asked to do something unconscionable, we draw on our ideals, values, and beliefs about how the world should be, and we make our choices accordingly. We may use ritual or prayer to support our response to challenges. When all these dimensions are accessible to one another, our experience feels satisfying and energizing, and we can more easily navigate new challenges.

In figure 3.3, we saw how each new dimension grows out of and encompasses previously developed dimensions and how our development alternates between an inner focus and an outward focus. We begin with the sensory-motor experiences of an infant, then add other stages of development. We use the reflective capacity in complex thinking to gain access to the psyche, with its dreams and imagination, then add values and ideals sometimes accessed through archetypal images, and finally land in the most comprehensive of all—the spiritual dimension. Each dimension brings new perspectives and capacity that can be used to solve the previously unsolvable problems embedded in what came before.

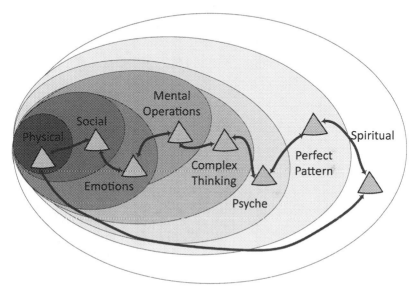

Figure 3.4 Dimensions in a Pattern of Organization.

Figure 3.4, as does figure 3.3, shows each dimension, but in this image, each is depicted as a component of the organizational pattern of our whole being. If we truly maintain a self-organizing pattern, we decide which dimensions need support and how we can best support them. We also make the call about what we will draw upon first in different challenging situations, and move ourselves from a focus on one dimension to another as needed and as possible. These connections among dimensions are crucial, not just because they provide the structure that allows us to build new capacity, but because that structure also allows us to discard what is not needed and supports the solving of our problems. This brings us to the dissipative structure—our third life quality, which is the focus of chapter 4.

Key Points

- We can only accommodate information that has some basis in what we already know.
- Accommodating new information requires that we disrupt our previous way of organizing in order to include what is new.
- Each newly developed dimension in anchored in previous dimensions.
- Dimensions can be seen as a spectrum of subtlety and complexity in human experiences, from what is tangible to our most subtle spiritual experience.
- Generally speaking, every dimension is available to every individual, and the more each is developed through experiences specific to that dimension, the greater its capacity to contribute to the person's sense of well-being.
- Each new dimension brings new perspectives that can help resolve problems raised in previous layers of development.
- Our ability to experience the sense of wholeness that is often associated with the sense of well-being depends on the connections among our different dimensions.

4 DISSIPATIVE STRUCTURE

In physics, the second law of thermodynamics tells us that everything is always drifting into a more chaotic state. As our environment becomes more erratic, we, as individuals, are naturally impacted by these changes. Our patterns of being and doing are disrupted again and again, yet we must try to function amid the chaos. Think about people who have survived a disaster, perhaps a car accident where personal injuries are sustained, and consider the mounting problems that sometimes follow. Loss of a job, bankruptcy, strained family relations, divorce, physical or emotional pain, and potential overuse of a narcotic are all possible fallouts from such an accident. If this person can't somehow manage to reorganize their priorities and their ways of doing things in the middle of or after such a major disruption, they will probably fall ill in one way or another and will die sooner than they would have had the accident not happened. This is all promised by the second law of thermodynamics according to its initial interpretation, and that truth has been proven many times. But not always. There is the *if* clause—if they can manage to reorganize themselves—so there is reason for hope.

New Interpretation of the Second Law of Thermodynamics

Physicists Ilya Prigogine and Isabelle Stengers came to a different conclusion about the impact of chaos for life systems. They found that sometimes in the trajectory of decline something occurs that helps the life system to reorganize itself into a new pattern and a new way to being and doing. If this new pattern is designed by the life system itself, it is a self-organizing pattern. It will include useful features presented by the chaos, and the new knowledge will be connected with existing experiences to make a bigger and more complex pattern. Because it will include features of the chaos, it will be more capable of meeting the challenge posed by that very kind of chaos. Prigogine and Stengers' work is referred to as the new interpretation of the second law of thermodynamics.[1] Their contribution brings a better understanding of the power a dissipative structure can have in shaping life into an experience of well-being.

For example, if the person in the car accident breaks a leg or sustains a head injury, the nature of these injuries will inform their habits and routines and how they see themself in terms of the capacity to go forward. Plans for the future may or may not be changed. In many cases, people in this kind of situation can make a few adjustments to accommodate the injury and resume some if not all of the same activities they enjoyed before the accident. However, those who experience a serious or prolonged illness must reorganize themselves in a fundamental way that transforms them into a different way of being.[2]

People who adapt to a chronic illness instead of fighting it can develop a new relationship with their bodies that is realistic given their new circumstance. According to Kathy Charmaz, adaptation means making accommodations for the new limitations so that the unity between body and identity is restored. In other words, people who adapt to a chronic illness shift their identity to more accurately match their body's current capacity. In a study conducted by Charmaz, research participants who were able to do this learned to see and use the strengths still available to them. Even as some physical capacities diminish, they learned to respond to new bodily cues that call for self-care. Being able to do this allowed a growing sense of self-efficacy and a reduction in fear of the unknown, in spite of new limitations.[3]

Adaptation is a primary feature of self-organization because it is internally driven and pulls together internal resources to meet the current challenge. It is a form of self-care in times of stress. It allows us to alter *how* we do things when *what* we can do is otherwise limited. Because it keeps the individual with chronic illness or a disability participating in life's activities, adaptation allows injured or ill individuals to present themselves as strong and resilient. When chronically ill research participants were realistic about their physical challenges, they were able to open to other dimensions of experience and to take on new roles accordingly, sometimes these chronically ill people were able to add the capacity to provide comfort to the healthy people around them.[4]

It seems that these kinds of changes might generate new respect in the tone of social responses to the chronically ill person, and perhaps with that, new opportunities for social networking and support. When resignation rather than adaptation is more prominent, such respect and cooperation would not be elicited. Adaptation, however, can shift the probability that an individual will enjoy a richer life with a greater sense of belonging and efficacy, regardless of chronic illness.

Like those with chronic illness or disability, people who are victims of domestic abuse, who are incarcerated, who are marginalized due to racism, or who otherwise experience oppression may also find that each and every intentional act to self-organize is important. Damaging patterns that are imposed over a long period of time are not easily uprooted and replaced, so every single act of self-care is important. As well as attending to immediate needs, each such enactment of self-care builds self-trust, which is vital to the healing of those who have suffered at the hands of others. When facing an oppressor, however, there can be danger in self-care. Difficult choices must be made regarding the risk-cost ratio of any efforts to self-organize. I am sure that people in the populations mentioned above recognize this.

Those who are oppressed must adapt constantly in order to stay alive and as healthy as possible. Viktor Frankl writes that when he was imprisoned at Auschwitz, he was initially overwhelmed by mundane thoughts, such as how he might acquire his next cigarette or a shoelace. Soon, however, the reflective and complex thinking skills he had used as a psychiatrist made it possible for him to analyze his situation and create a different response—one that literally kept him alive.[5] This is my point. As we become more aware of and adept in the possibilities our various dimensions offer, the more useful they can be in times of trouble. Frankl altered his initial response to imprisonment to a response that held more meaning. Although it would be a long stretch to suggest the remainder of his time in the camp was satisfying, it seems reasonable to say that it was more satisfying than was his time focusing on trivial things.

To be clear, I do not mean to suggest that adaptation to oppression is a desirable end goal. Nor do I mean that someone with a chronic illness or disabling condition should give up hope for better function or better health. Quite the contrary. Adaptation does not suggest giving up hope at all. It means working with what is in order to achieve an improved sense of well-being. In the moment, adaptation can save lives, and in the longer term, when we look at the fact that it is a primary feature of self-organization, we can also say that adaptation makes possible a fuller, healthier life in spite of any circumstance. This is what dissipation in human experience can look like—taking a bad situation and dealing with it in a way that expands our capacity to live life to the fullest extent possible.

In the previous chapter, we looked at how we select what information we will incorporate into our experiential bank, and how we reject what will not support us. The dissipative structure is integral to this process. It also acts as a clearinghouse for what has previously been incorporated into the pattern but no longer serves us. Experiences are incorporated because their interpretation aligns with the current identity of an individual. However, as that identity shifts to accommodate a new focus or new set of priorities, some of what was previously incorporated may get in the way. Old beliefs, old ways of thinking, or old habits may need to be set aside to make room for new beliefs, thought processes, and habits that better support the expanding capacity. Our conscious and subconscious choices about what we will hold on to and what we will let go of is indeed a process of transformation through occupation.[6]

Time

In human experience, the nuts and bolts of dissipation are complex and nuanced. Significant change requires time and reflection, even when boiled down to a specific and quick event. Because time is required, it will help to look at the sequence of transformative events. In figure 4.1, the smaller circles on the left represent the original pattern which is disrupted by an event. The middle, medium-size circles show the disrupted pattern of organization. Toward the right, as time goes on, there is additional input either from the external world or from inner dimensions. These are depicted, respectively, at the top and bottom of the diagram.

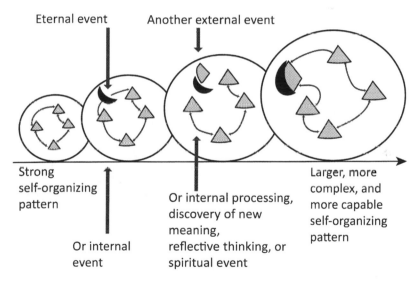

Figure 4.1. Equilibrium, Disruption, and Creative Expansion.

In order to accept and use that additional input, it must be considered in terms of the present components which are in a state of disarray. Though it may feel difficult, benefits of the disarray are multiple. The disruption of connections among components allows each component to be assessed for relevance to current needs. Simply adding a new experience or bit of knowledge to the mix without re-looking at what is there may only create further chaos. Assessment and management of the old is as important as assessment of and decisions about the new.

The sequence of internal events displayed in figure 4.1 does not occur in isolation. The external input may or may not be useful. If it is not, it will likely add to the experience of chaos. Furthermore, external input does not arrive only at a specific point on the timeline as shown in this figure. Two or more events, either internal, external, or both, can occur simultaneously. We might receive bad news on or close to the same day we fall ill. Or we might be in the state of disorganization from one event when people who are trying to be helpful load us with their perspective on what we should or should not have done or what we should or should not do. I discussed the harmfulness of this kind of helping earlier, and now we get a closer look. Imagine an addition to figure 4.1 that shows two disorganized individuals colliding, both of whom can be considered an external event that is disruptive to the other. This happens all the time, so it is important to fully understand how we can make navigational choices that will be truly helpful to all concerned.

To see more clearly what a dissipative structure looks like and how it works, I'll first describe it as a whole and then will give more details about the structures of inner life that support dissipation. I will also describe the structures of community life systems and how they support our safety and health.

The Structure

A structure always has components that are somehow in relation to one another. A building has a foundation, walls, a floor, and a ceiling. These are all functionally connected, with each serving its own purpose toward creating a building that is trustworthy. The structure of a life form is found in the components of its pattern of organization and in how these are connected with one another. When we make connections among our experiences, there is more possibility for coherence in our expressions about who we are and what we think and feel and need. When our experiential components are not connected, how we express ourselves—our identity—is compromised. We can do and say things that don't make sense to other people and it is more difficult to get our needs met.

In a conversation with Fritjof Capra, Stanslov Grof suggested that mental health hinges more on how people can integrate an experience or thought with their other experiences than it has to do with the actual content of that experience or their interpretation of it.[7] In other words, how we position each new experience in our minds in relation to our other experiences is more important than the content of any single experience.

We looked earlier at how the lack of self-organization can manifest in a tendency to reach outside oneself for support, and how this is not always a healthy option. It makes sense that when we cannot connect the dots between our experiences, we must reach outside ourselves for stability. Doing so is always evidence that we are in need of more internal stability. Given that self-organization underlies identity, self-expression, and coherence, Schaef's view that many kinds of mental illness fall into the addiction rubric makes makes sense.[8] Again, we see that to solve a problem in any of these areas we must look always to the self-organizing pattern.

To understand the dissipative structure better, we need more detail about the relationships among pattern components. In some ways these relationships will depend on the nature of the components. If we are looking at patterns of habits and routines, then we need to look for what holds our habits and routines together. For example, a person may have a habit of eating breakfast with a partner and then running off to work. If that person wants to maintain a partnership (social life) as well as nourish their body (physical life) and feed the bank account (outer-world life), then a bridge between breakfast and the rest of the day may be a meaningful glance, or word, or a kiss to secure the relationship until these partners can be in the same space again. It may be that no matter what happens at work, problems can be navigated more easily because there is that subtle connection with a loved one who cares.

This is the dissipative structure at work, choosing where we place focus and where we minimize our attention. The content of where we place our focus will grow in our minds. We will see it in more detail and will think of it more often. When we think of our difficulties more often, they will color a larger portion of our conscious life and eventually may appear insurmountable. When we focus more on that nod of acknowledgment from a loved one that, too, will gain traction and territory in our minds filling us with the sense of being loved and supported. Habits that secure positive moments in our daily routine, however fleeting, are the reminders that inform us of love across hours, days, weeks, or even years.

In the breakfast and departure example above, there are social, physical, and financial concerns all wrapped up together in a few minutes of time. They are somewhat distinct from one another, yet they are all dependent upon each other. The breakfast supports the day's work, and the day's work supports the breakfast. The partnership supports the day's work and may also support the breakfast directly as well as indirectly. The breakfast no doubt supports the partnership also. It is easy to see from this scenario that our different dimensions, as well as our habits and routines, can be components of our whole pattern of human experience.

In terms used by scholars of occupation (remember that occupation refers to the broad spectrum of how we occupy ourselves), the breakfast routine is an activity that carries meaning. I will say much more about meaning later, but want to point out here that meaningful activity provides a context for simultaneously utilizing and nourishing multiple dimensions of experience. Why is that important? Let's think for a minute about interpreting the components of a pattern as dimensions of experience and how our dimensions can support one another to keep the pattern intact. These connections are a significant part of the dissipative structure.

Our physical bodies are made in such a way that we can ingest and assimilate nutrition and eliminate toxins and waste. But when the nourishment we need is not available, a comforting hug or hand can help us feel better, at least for the moment. This is one way to use one dimension to support another. The concept of nourishment carries meaning in both dimensions, and when one dimension is left without what it needs, providing support through another dimension can be helpful. Similarly, people who are lonely may eat more than is necessary for their physical health in an attempt to fill that gap. This doesn't work as effectively as the other way around because social needs are more complex than physical needs. Furthermore, feeding a body that is not in need of food can create other problems, while filling a physical need with social support (temporarily) carries no complications. In fact, social support may bring other resources besides hand-holding to a hungry person.

Similar dynamics can be seen in other situations where different dimensions of experience share a theme of meaning. Struggles in understanding mental operations can be supported by expression of frustration (emotional dimension) or by reflective (complex mental) thinking. Expressing frustration won't necessarily solve a problem of mental operations but may relieve stress enough to allow thoughts to flow more freely. Reflection can add perspective and potentially open up new ideas about resources that might be used to resolve the problem.

Physicist and philosopher David Bohm believed that there is order in the connections among everything in the universe, including among the subtle and tangible realms of human experience. His search for understanding about the relationship between mind and matter was complemented and supported by his search for understanding about the relationship between particle and field as they are described in quantum science. Grounded in the implications of quantum physics, he identified an implicate order that underlies and can potentially explain everything we see as real in the outer world, including perceived incongruencies.[9] He conceptualized a series of energetic fields of increasing frequencies that are expressed as physical (tangible), mental (subtle), and spiritual (more subtle) experiences. Although there is a conceptual difference between the physical and subtle fields, these are merged, as are all fields, through a series of intermediary fields between them.[10]

To understand this concept, we must step away from the Newtonian-Cartesian thinking that wants to place distinct parameters around each object or concept. To serve our purposes here, we can use the concept of color to bring us to a new way of thinking. A rainbow has a discrete series of seven hues. However, between red and orange is an infinite number of combinations that create the defining line between them. Except for the very central point where red and orange are equally represented, there are many other colors where orange participates more and red less, in increasing degrees, or where red participates more and orange less in increasing degrees.

Because colors provide a familiar way to visualize different wavelengths, it makes sense to use this image to wrap our Newtonian-Cartesian minds around the concept of a series of waves of increasing frequencies. Although we speak of different colors as though they are discrete, they do not have discrete boundaries. Nor do the wavelengths that they reflect have discrete boundaries. Just as red participates with orange in varying degrees to create some version of red-orange or orange-red, our physical body participates in varying degrees with our social dimension to create some version of social transaction that is either more physical or more social. Those intermediary fields in human experience provide the context for the participation that informs the relationships among all our dimensional components and that allows for our sense of wholeness.[11] This is the essence of the connection among dimensional components that forms the human dissipative structure.

If we add emotion to our example of participating physical and social dimensions, then the participation is extended further, making the dissipative structure larger and more capable. If, for instance, there is a strong emotional pull to move toward or avoid something in the social world, participation between the emotional and social dimensions will inform how the physical transaction manifests. If the emotional pull to avoid carries more meaning than the social benefits of remaining engaged, manifestation may be a mixed bag of engagement, with the ultimate result being some kind of distancing. If the emotional pull to avoid is not honored in spite of its strength, this person will likely feel internal conflict and may say or do things that are not clear or consistent. Furthermore, if we hold back expression of a strong emotion, the dissipation that would otherwise be possible through manifestation will not occur, and that emotion will fester. It is when all dimensions work together that we feel most whole and healthy.

Although I have described dimensions as linearly related (and this will be useful when we discuss manifestation of our intentions), any dimension can be called upon to participate at any time, as long as that dimension is active and in resonance with what is happening. Calling upon adjacent dimensions may be easiest but that does not mean that non-adjacent dimensions cannot be tapped for participatory support. In terms of structure, remember that each dimension is imbedded in a more complex dimension. This means there are direct relations among all dimensions. The network among them is vast. Using it keeps us functioning as whole and healthy beings.

Dissipation in Individual Human Experience

When we shift our focus from a single dimension to multiple dimensions, several things occur. The vibratory frequency that characterizes that experience is shifted. This means that in addition to altering our inner experience, the new resonance we create will draw to us a different kind of experience. In other words, we will draw experiences to us that carry a different vibratory pattern than what was reflected with the singular dimension of experience.

I discussed previously the value of developing and including the more complex and encompassing dimensions in our lives. When we do this, we raise the vibratory frequency of our experience to a more subtle and complex pattern. This means that we will be more open to engaging with that which carries a higher frequency in our environment. Every time an individual raises his or her own vibratory pattern by adding new perspectives, the person's resonance attracts a higher frequency in others, and the resonance of the group will rise accordingly.

When we use our mental capacity to influence emotional distress, in addition to changing the vibratory frequency, mental focus also changes the experience, just as adding orange to red changes the hue of what we perceive. Raw emotion can be cradled in and through the participation of mental activity and will be altered in that safer environment. Cradling allows us to actively care for what is uncomfortable. In this way, adding perspective to an experience is another form of self-care because it brings the possibility of incorporating a more positive tone into the experience.

Many people interpret the edict to focus only on what is positive as a mandate to *not* take care of what is problematic but instead to look away toward what is more pleasant, as though the problem doesn't exist. Looking away, however, does not necessarily change the essence of the existing vibratory pattern, because it doesn't help us resolve the problem. Our capacity remains the same. And if avoiding what is hurtful is rooted in fear, that vibratory pattern will continue to draw similar experiences until the fear is prominent enough to demand our attention and a different response. We can cut to the chase by adding new dimensions that are relevant when a problem first arises. In this way of thinking, focusing on the positive is not really about sticking our head in the sand or looking away, but rather about adding enough perspective to give us the possibility of rising above our problems long enough and in a way that can actually support their resolution.

Participation of Dimensions

Bohm's idea that different dimensions of human experience participate with one one another[12] is key to dissipation. Completely switching focus from emotional content to mental activity does not support dissipation, because although the mental focus may be more complex, the possibility of stagnation is not eliminated. Change occurs only during and through transactions. In order to complete a transaction, participation is required. We must engage with our environment in order to live, and to do that we must include more than one dimension of ourselves. Ideas lead to action when there is an emotional impulse to manifest a change. That alone engages mental, emotional, and physical dimensions.

The infinite layers of differentiation between two dimensions is what makes interdimensional transactions possible. For example, when we dream, we can think about the dream upon awakening and then go about our day without further concern. Participation between the psyche and mental dimensions in this case is limited to one brief transaction, with no apparent incorporation of what the dream expressed nor any apparent influence on our dream life as a result of mental activity. The bulk of focus remains in the psyche where the dream occurred because there is little transaction with the mental dimension that might facilitate a change.

In another scenario, we might awaken with questions about the meaning of the dream, spend a few minutes coming up with some ideas, and again set it aside. In this case, there is more participation from the mental dimension, but the psyche continues to carry the load with not much more opportunity for change than in our first scenario. We could also waken from a dream, reach for our journal, and write extensively about our thoughts and feelings regarding the dream experience. In this scenario there is more participation from our mental and even emotional dimensions, and this brings more potential for change in our self-knowledge, our experience, and our ability to use our psyche to solve future problems as they arise.

At still another level of participation, we might begin our reflective process while in the dream state. This happens when a dream experience occurs and we have thoughts and feelings about the content right there in the dream that are consistent with the kind of thoughts and feelings we would have in our waking state. When we awaken, we can naturally extend this content through reflection and writing, but our mental dimension is already participating even before the dream ends. Conversely, we can reach into our dream world (imagining would be one way of doing this) to invite participation of our psyche in our conscious thought processes.

When Charmaz's research participants adapted to their illness or disability,[13] I believe they were reaching into their psyche dimensions for creative ideas that were then brought to fruition through the inclusion of thinking through what would work and what would not. I believe an emotional pull guided those participants toward choices that were interesting and pleasurable, and that took into account their physical and social needs as well as the capacity of others. The creative impulse may have arisen from a value of connection or service or something else. In this way, garnering participation among dimensions literally extended lives as well as improving life satisfaction. The adaptation provided the means for dissipation of distress.

We speak of different dimensions for the purpose of discussion and to deepen our understanding of the value of each and every aspect of who we are, but the dissipative structure *is* the whole and will function as a whole to the degree that it is able. That ability is determined by the intactness of each dimension and its capacity to participate with other dimensions, and this is what determines our ability to assimilate what is useful and to reject what is not.

Of particular importance is our social dimension, because it provides access to the various communities to which we belong. Just as each dimension brings a unique gift to an individual, each person brings something of value to a community's identity and function and to its ability to assimilate what is useful and reject what is not. Too often, communities reject what is different with little or no understanding of what is being offered or how it might be incorporated into existing community patterns. We know that an individual must resonate in some way with new information that is presented. Similarly, a community must resonate in some way with the unique gifts brought forth by an individual. Without that resonance, those gifts cannot be incorporated into community patterns.

Resonance may occur when one individual within a community finds a thread of similarity with what arrives from external sources. That individual can build understanding and share what has been learned with other community members who trust the individual. Resonance may also occur if an uncomfortable difference is interpreted as an opportunity to reach into oneself to discover the meaning behind the the discomfort.[14] Again, one individual's response of this nature can subsequently inform other community members if the resonance can be shared. These individual responses to distress are crucial to community processes because they introduce new capacity to the community's patterns of thinking and doing. Perspectives that challenge orthodox or common patterns of thinking can be frightening, not because they are in themselves harmful, but because they disrupt existing patterns. When one person in a community is able to find resonance with a challenging view, there is potential for flexibility and development of new community capacity.

A more legitimate danger to individuals and communities, though, are patterns that are not flexible or open to new perspectives but require absolute adherence to orthodoxy and demand allegiance to ideas and policies that do not support the four qualities (self-organizing pattern, process of cognition, dissipative structure, and meaning) that uphold life. In short, inflexibility and barring new ideas short circuits the process of cognition and cannot ultimately be satisfying or sustainable.

PATRICIA GAILEY, PH.D.

Dissipation in Community Affairs

A dissipative structure at the community level is comprised of components (community members) and the connections among them. We can think of this in much the same way that we think of the components in any life system—all components are equally important, and each has its own unique contribution. Each component or member of a community is developed to the degree possible, and some have more capacity than others. Because components of a community are individuals, the amount of experience each has in different dimensions determines what talent or skill they have to offer to the community. Whether it be emotional support, knowledge about something in particular, spiritual companionship, or caregiving, each member's contributions add something significant to the community's capacity as a whole. These contributions also inform how the community is perceived by others because the community identity is a direct reflection of the capacity of participating individuals.

The connections among community members, including but not limited to what they talk about among themselves, also informs the community's identity because connections are what support the potential to manifest ideas and solve problems. Enacting potential in these ways is a form of self-expression, and self-expression is the means by which we inform others of who we are in terms of value priorities and skills. *How* we interact with other community members determines the degree of participation possible among members and the strength of the community's dissipative structure. Simply adding one's own contribution is not enough. All that was said about self-knowledge, integrity, respectfulness, and authentic authority is applicable here because it is in those person-to-person communications that strong connections are made. So we must be clear about what we are adding and at the same time be open to the ideas expressed by others.

Refer back to the two circles in figure 2.1 (see chapter 2), where both depict a self-organizing pattern. Communications that come directly out of self-knowledge can be received by others without triggering fear because there is no indication of a need to manipulate, coerce, or otherwise control others. They create a certain ease for cooperating or collaborating toward common goals and toward resolving problems the community is experiencing. Leaders may use their roles of authority to inspire, direct, or inform, but it is largely through the direct communications among individuals that problems are solved. Someone says a kind word or reaches out to a person in need. Two people talking, playing around with ideas, come up with a strategy to solve a problem. They may try it out on a small scale, or invite others to consider exploring that idea. However, the agreement of two people does not mean the idea is good for everyone, particularly if other cultures are present in the community but not included in that private conversation. To assure that the idea will work for everyone, all perspectives must be considered, and this is accomplished through many conversations among many people. Indeed, sharing thoughts with the entire community can foster the emergence of new ideas that are viable for everyone.

But ideas of change must be supported by appropriate policy changes if they are to take root. This suggests that communication among leaders and community members must also be clear—as shown in figure 2.3 (see chapter 2). The metaphor of alternating left and right sides to keep ourselves balanced as we walk is useful here also, particularly if we recall that the pivoting action of the upper torso on the hips similarly coordinates the upper and lower body action. For dissipation in a community to be effective, the self-organizing ability of each and every member is key, and lines of communication among members and between members and leaders must be robust. Clear communications among members and leaders will naturally support the consideration of new perspectives required for solving problems because people will feel safe with one another.

For any given problem, failure to attend to and accommodate different perspectives can only result in a continuation of the view that fostered development of that problem, and therefore cannot solve it. New policies generated without incorporating new perspectives will not resolve the problem. In fact, because the community's process of cognition is not fully supported, the well-being of the community will likely falter, *even as those new but narrow policies are touted as good boundaries designed to protect the well-being of the community.*

Failure to listen to some voices is a certain pathway to exacerbating divisiveness among community members. This raises the question of how an individual can develop an authentic and unique identity by adding new perspective to the person's own base of knowledge while maintaining a sense of belonging in the context of a community that is reluctant to give up current patterns of being and doing. And if those current patterns reflect a unique community identity, how can they be maintained and at the same time be open to new perspectives offered by individuals who are evolving?

We saw how difficult it is sometimes for one person to incorporate a new perspective. For a community, it is all the more difficult because that new perspective is often delivered by one individual, replete with their own motives, intentions, sensitivities, shortcomings, and likely a unique set of experiences. In the case of one person incorporating new information, we saw some kind of resonating match is required. It is no different when an individual seeks to belong in a certain community. Here, the resonance, which is the way in, may be discovered in a conversation with one or two individuals in the community. But again, if communications are not clear—if the true identity of the community or individual is misrepresented—then the resonance will fall flat sooner or later, and the relationship will be compromised.

As with individuals, expression of the community's identity must be based on self-knowledge. A community's self-knowledge resides in its individual members. Therefore, it can be expressed by individuals who are aware of community history, shared values, and experiences, as well as in expressions designed collaboratively such as occurs in a community motto, tourism themes, or claims of successes in navigating commonly held concerns. Community self-knowledge that has been attained through the process of identifying shared values and ideals will naturally demonstrate an increased capacity to solve problems. The resulting clarity in values and priorities will speak through policies in all aspects of governance. However, when self-knowledge is not attended, internal conflicts among factions of the community will quickly develop and communications at all levels of authority will be compromised.

Coupling community self-knowledge with an open mind to what other communities have to say about themselves fosters individual communication across community boundaries as well as fostering group to group communications. Being open to another's ways of being and doing can be instructive. This does not mean we should all go out and adopt the cultural practices of others without taking time to learn and appreciate what knowledge those practices embody. That said, sharing ideas for coping can further individual dissipation of issues or trauma, and can serve to bring communities together.

Lastly, learning about another person's current and historical experiences as well as population experiences across the centuries adds depth to our understanding of the true nature of justice and injustice. It cannot hurt to further one's process of cognition. The only pain is in potentially giving up unhealthy practices, or as Kendi describes, policies that lock us into inflexible and unsustainable patterns.[15] It makes sense to be proactive, to take the bull by the horns, and to challenge ourselves with this difficult task rather than waiting for the entropy surrounding us to take its toll.

Naturally, we each participate with others and in community affairs to varying degrees and for different reasons. One identity we claim does not necessarily interfere with any other, though it might. Hamad's Danai (see chapter 1) in *White Tears/Brown Scars* experienced a conflict as she attempted to develop her professional identity because her racial identity was not embraced in a positive way by her work group. The dissonance presented an internal conflict that had to be resolved in order to restore her sense of balance and satisfaction.

The decisions made by Danai are also pertinent to community dissipation. Her ultimate focus on her own identity as a Black woman no doubt contributed to other Black women and to the community of Black women. In being true to her own identity and needs, she potentially strengthened communications among Black women while halting the dysfunctional communications at her workplace. The problems in her workplace were not resolved, but Danai could not address them by herself. She needed a partner with whom she could participate in meaningful conversation in order to initiate change. No individual in her work group was available for that, nor would her employer have supported such a partnership. Danai's move to connect with other Black women placed her in a position in which there was a greater possibility for experiencing a sense of belonging as well as for manifesting justice.

The key is to forge authentic connections where these are possible and to limit participation in connections that are not authentic. When authentic connections bring people together in action, those bonds will be strengthened through participation. And again, participation is what makes dissipation possible. It is through doing things together, collaborating so that the gifts of each can be incorporated into what is manifested, that problems are solved and new capacities can emerge.

We previously looked at how individuals' distress requires reaching into a more complex dimension in order to reestablish a self-organizing pattern. Because communities are by definition complex, community issues and trauma will require an even more complex and subtle dimension of experience in order to reestablish a self-organizing pattern for the community. This means that at least some community members must have capacity developed beyond the complex and reflective thinking that supports societies and organizations. It will be the imaginative, creative dream world, and collective unconscious potential of the psyche that will provide the perspective and ideas that can better organize the experience of clashing systems of thought.

Leaders who have developed their psyche dimension through dream work or creative efforts would be optimal. However, given the current and historical requisite that leadership focus on sociopolitical affairs, an elected leader with developed capacity in the psyche dimensions is not likely. On the other hand, a prevailing practice among community members of looking more deeply into ourselves and of sharing meaning in a way that invites the full participation of others in creative activities would be a step in the right direction. Such activities would inform any community response to issues or trauma as well as forging the connections that support life.

Some people and communities can use their dissipative structures fluently, navigating challenges with relative ease and gaining capacity for new ways of being and doing in the process. We think of these people as resilient. Resiliency brings to mind an image of a healthy, highly engaged individual who can call upon multiple dimensions of experience and successfully engage in transactions with others. It is time now to explore those transactions in more detail and to consider the implications they have for our sense of well-being. For this, we turn to meaning, which is the fourth quality required for life.

Key Points

- Adaptation and personal growth are key to an ongoing sense of well-being.
- A dissipative structure consists of the components of a life system and, perhaps more importantly, how they connect with one another.
- New perspectives discovered as dimensions are added to one's experience are key to solving problems that seemed previously unsolvable.

- In one individual, or in a community, the different dimensions of experience simultaneously relevant to an activity can be said to participate with one another as that activity unfolds.

- Networks of shared identity in various levels and arenas of community provide the wherewithal for connections that support dissipation of community issues and trauma.

- New ideas can emerge when community members participate together to solve problems.

- Clear communication among all community members, including leaders, is necessary to the ability of the community to enhance its capacity and to solve problems.

- A bigger perspective is often required in order to solve community problems, and because communities are already complex systems that bigger perspective might be available in exploration of the psyche dimension.

- Cultural and community influence can only support well-being if norms uphold the four qualities that support life.

5   MEANING

The fact that Viktor Frankl could draw on his psychiatric experience to reorganize his patterns of thinking and doing are evidence that his dissipative structure was still serviceable in spite of the incredible harm being done at Auschwitz. He began paying attention in a different way. Instead of focusing on the mundane, he noticed how assaults perpetrated by the Nazis impacted him and his incarcerated comrades.[1] By shifting his focus, he refused to allow others to define him and instead brought more of his developed capacity to bear on the situation. What he learned from his experience was that meaning is crucial to ongoing life.

Capra and Luisi argue that the meaning of anything is found in its relationship with context.[2] Indeed, Frankl changed his relationship with Auschwitz and the Nazi regime by focusing on the larger perspective available in his role as a psychiatrist.[3] Each of us, lover or warrior, oppressed or oppressor, comrade or loner, is in relationship with our context. Although there is always contextual pressure to play certain roles, we are in charge of how much of ourselves we bring to that relationship.

In the profession of occupational therapy, there is a foundational tenet that doing something meaningful is healing. Doing requires playing some kind of role—parent, custodian, teacher, salesperson, among others—that determines the nature of our participation. From a more universal perspective, we play different roles in our relationships with ourselves and others. In their book *An Occupational Perspective of Health* Wilcock and Hocking use the terms doing, being, belonging, and becoming to discuss the meaning in occupation with regard to health. These words characterize our relationship with context. We are active participants (doing), simply present (being), sure of our connection with others around us (belonging), or changing as a result of our transactions (becoming). Hasselkus sees meaning as derived from our desire to make sense of what we experience.[4] Not so different from understanding our relation with our context, this perspective brings focus to how we are able to organize what we learn in the course of our participation, so that we can access it at a later time.

In Frankl's story, his ability to act (doing) in a way that expressed his capacity as a psychiatrist was grossly disrupted by his incarceration, but because the capacity itself was still intact, he was able to find a new way to participate in the concentration camp context. He identified himself as a doctor and this opened the door for him to participate in ways that would not have been otherwise possible. This new way of being and doing was more satisfying than his focus on the mundane and ultimately allowed him to contribute something unique to the world. Making that shift in his relationship with his context was similar to the shift in Charmaz's chronically ill research subjects. In both cases, the reality of the situation was acknowledged and adaptations were made that allowed individuals to develop new patterns that took the new contextual information into account.[5]

Before we can understand how to transform our relations with our context, we need to know more about what relationship entails. This is precisely what David Bohm explored in his 1990 paper entitled "A New Theory of the Relationship of Mind and Matter" and his 1985 book entitled *Unfolding Meaning: A Weekend of Dialogue with David Bohm*. He was intrigued by several properties of quantum science and believed that understanding those properties might shed light on our understanding of human experience. He used his interpretations of those properties to develop an understanding of human experience and the relations between body and mind and between humans and their contexts.[6]

Quantum Properties and Meaning

When we consider even the tiny components of an atom, depending on the observation tool, we will see either a wave or a particle. The context is the observation tool and this is what determines our interpretation of what is seen. The lens (context) we use to look at a human also determines what we will see. If we use our physical eyes or some extension of our eyes (X-ray or microscope, for example), we see a human body with all its organs, senses, and physical capacity. If we look at a human under the lens of a lifetime of changes, we will see a vibrant bundle of experiences that make up that person's history, perspectives, and desires. If we choose to use cultural and community norms as a lens, we will see a person's identity and potential for participation—who they are, what their capacity for participation and contribution is, what roles they play, and where they belong.

Wave or Particle, Field or Body, and Meaning

Most physicists who studied the inner workings of the atom in the early years of quantum science chose to focus on either the particle view or the wave view. Bohm didn't want to limit his knowledge to one or the other. He wanted to understand the relationship between the two, because he thought it might shed light on the relationship between the mind (the subtle) and matter (the tangible) aspects of human experience. Bohm began his inquiry by looking for something shared by both particle and field, a common denominator that would help him understand their relationship. What he found is that the *information* that guides the shape of the wave also guides the shape of the particle.[7]

In classical physics, the influence of a wave is determined by its intensity. For example, a rock thrown into a pond creates ripples proportionate to the size of the rock. In quantum science, the influence of a quantum field (the same thing as a wave) is determined by the information it carries. Figure

5.1 below shows how a particle, depicted as a pentagon, is one view of a five-sided figure, and the five-sided wave or field is another view. They are both expressions of the same meaning.[8]

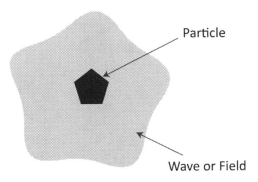

Figure 5.1. Particle-Field.

In terms of human experience, Bohm suggested that meaning is the *information* that guides our thoughts and beliefs, our ideas and our values, our words and behavior, *and* what we bring into manifestation in the most tangible sense. In other words, the meaning held in our minds *informs* our tangible experience.[9] The form of our thoughts—be they placid or violent, constructive or damaging—informs our tangible words and behavior. Conversely and simultaneously, our tangible experiences with the outer world—be they placid or violent, connecting or isolating—inform our feelings, thoughts, values, and spiritual life. Bohm describes a constant unfolding and enfolding flow of *informing* so much so that we may not realize that what is in our environment was always in our mind, and vice versa. This is congruent with the argument raised by Maturana and Varela that we only see what is in ourselves already.[10]

E = mc² = Meaning

Another quantum property states that all action is in the form of energy, or quanta (from which the name quantum physics is derived). The term quanta describes indivisible energy packets, each with its own vibrational frequency. A quantum field is sometimes called a quantum potential because it carries some degree of energetic potential for action. Bohm believed that because thought can be described as active information, it is a kind of action. and that it can also be interpreted as a kind of informing activity, or meaning.[11] He concluded that if action is a form of energy and meaning is a form of action, meaning must also be a form of energy.[12]

Indeed, this bears out in human experience. Confronted with something that holds meaning for us, a book, person, an upcoming event, or a memory, we perk up, pay attention, and experience an energetic lift that gives us the ability to act. Not surprisingly, communication is also equated with energy in the field of cybernetics.[13] The potential to act derived from communication that holds meaning is the very source of our doing. It also provides an energizing effect that makes us actually *feel* alive.

Bohm surmised that thought (active information) is what organizes human activity because the meaning inherent in the thought informs the activity. With active information in the mind manifesting in tangible activity, there is a sense of wholeness in which the experience of energy and vitality is intact. This is demonstrated in occupational science research. When individuals are not able to carry out ideas that are meaningful, they experience a depletion of energy.[14] In other words, it appears that blocks between thoughts and their trajectory into actions results in loss of energy because the meaning that links subtle and tangible forms is disrupted.

Conversely, when individuals *are* able to carry out plans that hold meaning for them, their experience of vitality is robust. So when we organize ourselves to do an activity (self-organization musters all relevant dimensions of capacity), there is energetic potential to manifest those ideas.[15] The meaning in our mind that informs our actions serves as a common denominator that connects thought and action, maintaining the integrity of the whole person and thus their energetic potential. In fact, meaning is so much a source of energy that Bohm added a third leg to Einstein's $E = mc^2$ equation to read $E = mc^2$ = meaning.[16]

PATRICIA GAILEY, PH.D.

Non-Local Influence and Meaning

The idea of wholeness is integral to the system's view proposed by Capra and Luisi in which the four qualities that support life—the self-organizing pattern, the process of cognition, the dissipative structure, and meaning—are inextricably related to one another and together provide all that is necessary for life. The quality of meaning ensures that a life system has a relationship with its context and the context is full of living systems that nourish and support one another. In this way, there is always an outer world (a part of the whole system) that shapes and supports human life. The idea is that the connections among living systems together form a teaming network of vitality—a wholeness of the universe.[17]

Similar to that teaming network of vitality, Bohm envisioned the cosmos as a flowing process of enfolding and unfolding. His term soma-significance refers to enfolding meaning as knowledge about what has manifested rolls through increasingly subtle fields from physical (somatic) experience to thoughts and beyond (significance). His term signa-somatic refers to the unfolding of meaning as subtle fields of thought are realized in physical form. This is not so different from the process of cognition, where transactions within the larger network contribute to the development of our identity and expression.[18]

Some influences on human behavior fall outside what is possible to view through the Cartesian-Newtonian lens. Bohm wanted to understand more about causality—what causes things to happen. He wanted a scientific explanation, and he wanted his science to be useful. He thought about the idea of hidden variables for more than forty years.[19] His work eventually supported our understanding of non-locality, which can be described as the influence of one object on another regardless of space or time constraints. Bohm thought there was an invisible field of information that could guide behavior.[20]

Indeed, there are variables that shape our choices without our being aware of the influence. One example is trauma that is buried deep in memory, inaccessible to conscious thought, yet is known to affect emotions and behavior across a lifetime, particularly so while that person remains unconscious of the trauma. Bohm saw thought as a non-local influence on behavior.[21] Indeed, the effect of thought on behavior is not limited by the constraints of time and space.

The example mentioned earlier of cultural beliefs as an influence on individual behavior is used by Capra and Luisi and by Bohm to help explain meaning. Capra and Luisi's comments revolve around the idea that a culture is informed by the network of individual identities even as individual identities are informed by the cultural identity. Bohm's explanations are intertwined with wave-particle knowledge, wherein the meaning in cultural beliefs informs the behavior of those who are encompassed by that culture and the meaning in tangible experience informs thoughts and ideas that support the culture. The two views, although expressed slightly differently, are essentially the same in regard to meaning as the primary definer of relations between individual and context. Bohm also saw potential to apply this idea to relations among the subtle and tangible dimensions of one person, or to one life system, or to larger life systems.[22]

Our spiritual experiences, our values and ideals, dreams and imagination, and thoughts can be considered non-local influences because they inform our behavior. In a way, these more subtle dimensions provide a context within which our more tangible dimensions function. A spiritual experience can transcend time to inform our thoughts and actions for many years, as can a good or bad dream. Similarly, meanings construed from our interpretations of recalled memories can transcend time and space to inform us of subtle directives from friends or family, leaders, or ancestors regardless of their physical absence; and ethical and moral concerns all influence how we think and behave.

Dilemma

We are faced with a small dilemma to our understanding of wholeness and meaning. In developmental terms, a new dimension emerges from existing experiences as an entirely new perspective. The new perspective includes experiences that just wouldn't fit into the old patterns, and is organized according to that content, yet still encompasses the previously known perspectives. The new dimension is by definition larger and more capable. Valerie Hunt's research on consciousness and field frequencies supports this premise. Her research subjects who spent more time with subtle and refined content—those she identified as mystics and healers— had wave frequency signatures that were much more complex than the frequency signatures of people who engaged primarily in mundane tasks.[23] This means that the degree of complexity in our thoughts and actions is reflected in the degree of complexity in our vibrational patterns.

More to my point, though, is that the presence of a mystic or healer can have a profound organizing effect on the vibratory patterns of individuals whose auras (which can be interpreted as expressions of identity) are not well organized. The effect in Hunt's research was evident even when the scattered individual was not consciously aware of the presence of the mystic or healer. This means that a context (or contextual factor) that includes a stable complex vibratory field can and does inform those vibratory fields that are less organized in a way that brings them into greater stability.[24]

In contrast to the idea of expanding capacity as development occurs is that in none of Bohm's explanation of meaning does he suggest the potentiality of mind or matter is greater than the other. Yes, our more subtle dimensions do have power to hold sway over what our more tangible dimensions manifest, but our tangible experiences also inform our thoughts, dreams, values, and beliefs, changing us accordingly. This is equally powerful.

The dilemma, I believe, is in a Western culture inclination to judge some human experiences as more worthy than others. Perhaps our judgments are based on monetary gain, or emotional intensity, or novelty, and if one of these qualities is not present, I think we often diminish the value of the experience. This means we devalue the mundane in our minds, causing us to rush through tasks that could, if we were to pay attention, offer spiritual insight and growth. If appreciation for the inherent and metaphoric value of mundane tasks is not in our minds, we miss out entirely. But when mundane experiences are considered for their spiritual potential, it becomes difficult to separate what is mundane and what is spiritual. And that is the point.

Power is not in any single dimension, nor is it weighted at either end of the dimensional spectrum. When we divide ourselves by assuming that our ability in one dimension—be it mental, physical, spiritual, social (political or economic), or other—is superior to our other dimensions, we risk diminishing our power. But when we balance spiritual activities with the mundane and spend time reflecting, attending to our emotions, and thinking, we support our wholeness, which is our true source of empowerment.

Unfolding and Enfolding Meaning

In the previous chapter we looked at how different dimensions of experience can participate with one another in varying degrees. I have used the term resonance to suggest a similarity that would allow communication. More specifically now, resonance can be thought of as having a similar vibratory pattern or as shared meaning. Without shared meaning there is no commonality upon which to base communications. Participation is neither prompted nor energized. The idea Bohm expressed about wholeness in his "New Theory" article and in is book about unfolding meaning was that meaning is the common denominator that holds us all together, and it does so by prompting and supporting participation across the spectrum of human dimensions and with our outer world.

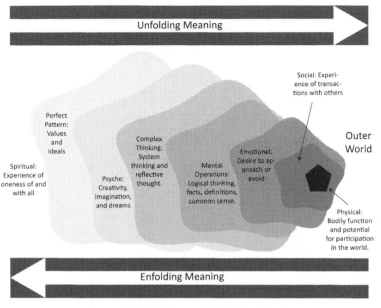

Figure 5.2. Unfolding and Enfolding Meaning.

Nonlocality substantiates that everything is connected. Bohm's conceptualization of the universe, which he called the Implicate Order, describes those connections. In the Implicate Order, the meanings in our subtle dimensions prompt a cascade of resonance and participation across increasingly tangible dimensions as our thoughts unfold into manifestation. Similarly and simultaneously, the meaning in tangible events, such as a car accident or birth of a baby, prompt participation through our subtle dimensions as they enfold back through the layers of our being.[25]

Consider figure 5.2, which expands on figure 5.1 to illustrate unfolding and enfolding fields of meaning across this sample of the dimensional spectrum, with increasing subtlety depicted as lighter shades. The dark pentagon, which represented a particle in figure 5.1, here represents a physical body. A brief description of the kind of meaning possible for each dimension is provided in figure 5.2. The arrows show the unfolding of meaning from subtle forms to manifestation, and the enfolding of meaning from tangible outer-world events through emotions, thoughts, dreams, and other subtle dimensions.

Of course, not all unfolding of meaning reaches manifestation. Plans go awry for a variety of reasons. Sometimes they are dropped in favor of other priorities. Sometimes they are halted because there is a lack of resonance in one or more dimensions. And sometimes our ideas must be laid aside because they receive no support from others in our community. And finally, what is my priority may be actively blocked by others as they attempt to prevent harm that could be caused by my oblivious intentions.

Hasselkus tells a story about a student therapist who was instructed to provide therapy for a nonresponsive individual—someone who actually died a few days after her visit. For this student there was a mismatch between her instructions and what was possible, so much so that she was "frozen" and unable to merge the disparate meanings in a way that would allow her to move forward.[26] It is only when there is resonance all the way through an individual's spectrum of relevant dimensions, from the most subtle point of origin to the tangible, and including resonance with others who are impacted, that ideas can fully manifest in a beneficial way.

Ideas do not always come from the depths of our being. I might decide to pursue a project I think will be of interest to others. Of course, the planning will require a certain amount of emotional investment and thought but probably won't reach much deeper unless my project is grounded in ethical or moral ideals or spiritual beliefs. If these are my grounding, then engaging the participation of the psyche dimension for its imaginative contributions, as well as complex thinking for its reflective capacity and multiple perspectives, will create a more robust experience of resonance and a degree of clarity that will make the project more likely to succeed.

Just as not all unfolding reaches manifestation or comes from our more subtle dimensions, not all enfolding reaches the depth of spiritual experience. If a visit to a loved one is cancelled, the effect may register briefly in emotional and mental dimensions, but the cancellation might be just a superficial blink in an otherwise busy schedule. If there is deeper meaning, however, such as an expectation that the meeting would meet a need for complex mental stimulation or refreshed hope, or if the loved one died before another contact could be arranged, then the cancellation would of course have more meaning in those subtler dimensions.

Meaning in Occupying Ourselves and Our Lives

Unfolding and enfolding occur in every occupation. This is the nature of occupation. No matter how we occupy ourselves, whether it be working on projects or visiting loved ones, parenting, gardening, or fulfilling a worker role, our participation unfolds the meanings in our minds into manifestation, and simultaneously enfolds the meaning of those manifestations to inform our emotions and thoughts, our imagination, and our dreams and values. This is my understanding of Bohm's theory about unfolding and enfolding as it is articulated in his writings I've already mentioned, and it is precisely echoed in Hasselkus's arguments that participation in occupations unfolds layers of meaning and that the action of doing prompts the realization of meaning.[27]

Key to understanding the power of meaning in occupation is that there are always multiple dimensions involved. We have looked at this many times already, but it bears repeating because acknowledging and understanding the complexity of the meaning in occupation provides a framework by which we can more accurately design our experience of well-being. We've learned that resonance in multiple dimensions provides the substance of connectivity among them that supports a pattern of dimensions working together. We've considered that activity in one dimension can stir participation in adjacent dimensions, thus fostering development of new perspectives and new capacity. We've seen how stress can be mitigated by involving more complex dimensions, by creating potential for meaning to manifest from subtle to tangible dimensions, and by fostering new learning and building capacity based on tangible experiences.

With this knowledge it is clear that meaning supports a self-organizing pattern, a process of cognition, and a dissipative structure, and that our occupations—defined as participating in activities which hold meaning— are key to supporting every quality required for the continuation of our lives and well-being. In figure 5.3 we see the arrows that in figure 5.2 indicate unfolding and enfolding, but now they are more accurately collapsed into one bidirectional arrow with the spectrum of dimensions represented along the shaft. For any identified occupation, a certain group of dimensions will be relevant. In different case examples these would be represented by different lengths of the arrow.

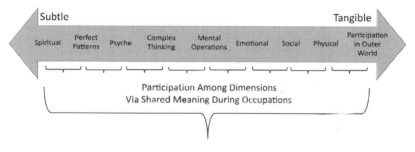

Improves strength of self-organizing pattern
Supports expansion into new realms of experience
Supports mitigation of stress
Suppots participation in outer world

Figure 5.3. Impact of Meaning in Occupations on Life Qualities.

I do not believe that adjacency is required for participation of any dimension or that those between the most subtle and the most tangible must necessarily be fully active. It is too easy to imagine situations in which multiple dimensions that are not adjacent participate together. For example, a moment of spiritual inspiration prompts a donation to a homeless person. I use the linear model because it is impossible for me to explain the vast network of connections that describe our human experience without serious oversimplification.

But what happens when those intermediary dimensions are not well developed or capable of supporting an initiative? In at least some cases, there could be a breach in how the meaning, the active informing aspect, plays out. If we are not able to garner social support for a project, then making it happen will be more difficult.

There is also the possibilities that our spiritual beliefs might support ideas that feel harmful to others who hold different spiritual beliefs. Not everyone believes that initiation rites are activities they want to embrace. Similarly, praying for someone who is hungry rather than sharing food resources might be offensive to the hungry person. If we can't develop a reasonable budget, then manifesting our project will be more difficult. If we can't physically do what we want to do, then, obviously, making it happen will be more difficult.

There is also a possibility of believing that an idea is spiritually based because of a flush of energy or an overwhelming desire to be helpful. These experiences could be prompted by a need to bolster one's own ego or a number of other kinds of imbalance. Having developed capacity in the middle region of the range of dimensions would tend to support the manifestation of a truly spiritual initiative, and would tend to quell an idea that is less optimally inspired.

Another potential problem is a mismatch among meanings, where held meanings carry opposing information. I alluded to this earlier in my mention of internal conflicts. Sometimes we have mixed feelings about manifesting an idea. Or we don't have enough information, or the best information, or a certain kind of social support, or perhaps our perspective is limited by certain values or beliefs. Any of these issues or others would diminish our overall potential for successful manifestation of an idea. Internal discord can make it difficult to follow any single focus. Obviously, when an individual is ill or has a disability, issues that disrupt the manifestation of ideas that are meaningful are more prevalent. This is where occupational therapy shines—in helping people to navigate their lives by matching abilities with tasks and with environmental factors so that manifestation is more easily possible.

Pentland and McColl define occupational integrity as the extent to which a person lives according to their values, capacity, and what is meaningful to them. They argue that living with occupational integrity is the best bet for experiencing a sense of well-being.[28] But this assumes that the values embraced are healthy values. Occupations that have an addictive quality may be motivating because they provide a sense of security where self-knowledge is not robust. For example, a person may be capable of making business deals that are lucrative in their occupation of generating wealth. They may feel good about supporting their family financially and be active members of a community, sitting on school boards, or active in the chamber of commerce or men's or women's clubs. But even as they live according to their values and capabilities and according to what holds meaning in their lives, their voice and actions may cut others off from much needed resources, thus creating relationship difficulties.

In their blog "Qualitative Growth," Capra and Henderson point out that unlimited economic growth is unsustainable and that turning our attention to the quality of our relational experience would be a better focus.[29] I would argue that, according to what we saw when we looked at relationships, focus on economic growth without attention to the quality of our lives *and the lives of those around us* is harmful to all concerned. The term unsustainable, especially when we accommodate to it, fails to convey the dirty truth that we hurt ourselves and others when we participate in patterns and processes that support financial gain rather than the four qualities that sustain life.

For example, when warrior ideals are applied to create financial gain, balance with other archetypes might quickly yield to the desire for monetary reward. So although developing warrior competence is commendable, Pearson tells us that the most advanced warrior fights for what really matters—which we know is what supports life. The anything-goes attitude embraced by a less developed warrior, and even a principled fight with altruistic intent (recalling that those who reach out to help might have insufficient boundaries) have potential to harm others. Similar statements can be made about any archetypal figure or ideal.[30]

Our task is to find ways to support the four qualities that will keep us alive and well. Every challenge we face provides an opportunity to re-create our self-organizing pattern in a healthier way while supporting others in their self-organizing efforts. If we pay attention, we can learn how make decisions that lead to more satisfying lives for everyone. During times when my own sense of well-being is less than optimal, I find it helpful to occupy myself with tasks that bring focus to the four qualities that support life. Letting my most subtle values inform my priorities, banking on self-organizing patterns combined with expanding perspectives on health and well-being, and finding ways to mitigate stress makes a tremendous difference to my sense of well-being.

Chapter 6 summarizes the previous chapters and provides suggestions about how we can make decisions that incorporate the necessary qualities into our ways of being and doing, belonging, and becoming.

Key Points

- Meaning is necessary to life and is always found in our relationship with context. Without it, human life cannot continue.
- Meaning (information) unfolds from our subtle to tangible dimensions, shaping how those tangible experiences manifest. It enfolds from the tangible experiences to the more subtle, changing our feelings, our thoughts, our values. and our beliefs.
- Activity with meaning (occupation) stirs an experience of energy.
- Meanings in subtle dimensions are more complex than meanings in tangible dimensions in both content and in energetic frequencies. That informing complexity can guide what is less complex and have a stabilizing influence on what is less well organized.

- Authentic and sustainable empowerment come from activation and use of a broad spectrum of dimensions in balance with one another.
- Participation of dimensions with one another is dependent on shared meaning among them. That shared meaning is a common denominator through which communication and collaboration can occur.
- Occupying ourselves with what is meaningful has potential to strengthen our self-organizing pattern, our process of cognition, and our dissipative structure, but only if our occupational choices support these life-sustaining qualities.
- Embodied experience in our everyday occupations is key to spiritual development because it informs our entire being of what supports life.

6 DECISIONS TO CONSIDER

The science presented in this book is one way to look at how we can construct and sustain satisfying lives. It can be applied to individual situations through reflection about each decision to determine if the four qualities required for life will be upheld by that decision. The same process can also be applied to community issues, including questions of social justice in all their various and complex forms.

In this chapter I review the four life qualities, adding more detail about the choices each quality presents us within our daily lives, and an invitation to choose a path that is life-sustaining and can be trusted to lead to a flourishing experience. I begin with the concept of individuals encompassed in layers of contextual arenas.

Each human is part of a social group that is part of a larger group that is part of a still larger group. Because groups require that we play certain roles, these expanding social contexts inform how we identify ourselves. Although we have little choice about who comprises our immediate family, and our family interactions may be steeped in long traditions, we do have a choice between following those traditions or breaking away from them.

- Consider doing both. Study your family patterns and history to learn more about those unseen ancestral forces that inform your ways of being and doing. If you see patterns that uphold any of these four life qualities (the self-organizing pattern, the process of cognition, the dissipative structure, or meaning), hang on to them! Emphasize them, and call other family members in to your new way of thinking and doing!

Within and beyond family, we have opportunities to choose our companions. Those choices either enable us to have the kind of relations that bring us closer to one another or, conversely, are disruptive to our self-organization and make healthy connections difficult to sustain. From the standpoint of what supports life are several considerations to make. Does a potential comrade treat us respectfully by listening carefully to what we say? Does this person show appreciation for who we are and the contributions we offer? Does this person speak and behave in a way that builds trust?

- Consider seeking out comrades who are themselves self-organizing and who appreciate your need to be self-organizing. Surround yourself with people who value what you value and appreciate your expressions of your unique identity.

We may or may not be able to choose which larger community we will call home. Some of us are locked into a social situation due to economic or occupational realities or social injustices, while others enjoy the privilege of more choice. Regardless, the kind of role you choose to play in your community is important. Which roles are a natural extension of your identity and capacities? Is your community open to what you have to offer? Do you find enough shared meaning to work toward manifesting the kind of community you want?

- Pay attention to whether your community roles and relations allow you to contribute what is authentically yours to contribute. Look for ways that your contributions can add to a community-level, self-organizing pattern by filling a community need, then set up lines of communication between yourself and other community members who play adjacent roles. Contribute your unique knowledge in a way that will increase your community's knowledge. A knowledgeable community will be better equipped to navigate social and ecological challenges.

One of the most fundamental choices we face is whether to assert our individuality or to conform to group norms. If we don't assert our individuality, it is easy to feel swept up into patterns that don't align with our morals and ideals. This can make us both vulnerable to harm and at risk for perpetrating harm on others. On the other hand, if we assert an individual perspective that differs from traditional community patterns we can quickly feel, if not actually *be*, isolated, which would diminish our sense of belonging and safety.

- Consider seeking balance between the two extremes. While finding a community with people who are open to most of what you have to offer seems optimal, it may not be feasible. Think about the different aspects of yourself and consider developing community ties with different groups to support those different aspects. This is probably not a new concept to most people—many of us have a workplace community, a faith-based community, and perhaps a leisure community also. Consider consciously seeking out communities that can support your expression and personal growth and use meaning—what resonates—as a connecting tool to foster a greater sense of belonging without compromising your integrity.

Self-Organizing Pattern

Our self-organizing pattern is comprised of our life experiences as we place them into a constellation that allows smooth operations, easy access to knowledge about each experience, and action with integrity. Our habits and routines are the components that make up the patterns of how we move through our days. At the same time, all the dimensions of our experience together are components of our being. These reflect our identity and determine our potential for participation. Patterns of doing and being support one another, shifting and expanding as new experiences are encountered.

- Consider developing, one by one, habits that carry a deeper meaning. For example, rather than pushing yourself to exercise just for the sake of exercise, try adding another dimension of benefit. Walk with a friend you want to get to know better, or listen to an audio book you've been wanting to hear, or use your exercise time for reflection or planning.

The shifts that occur as new experiences are incorporated are by definition disruptive to old patterns. These old patterns must be broken so that new and more capable patterns can be established. Because our patterns inform our identity and our boundaries, these disruptions can interfere in how we communicate with others. Attending to relationships while we care for ourselves can be a puzzle, especially when others are similarly challenged. Disruption in the wider community complicates matters further.

- Consider being vigilant in your awareness of your own processes— your relationship habits, in which dimensions of experience you primarily reside, and which patterns of doing and being you default to when you are challenged.

Self-care habits often take a backseat when times get tough. Pressing problems need our attention, so we skip meals, rest, or exercise routines. We think we will make it up to ourselves when we are under less stress. What many fail to recognize is that those stressful times are precisely when we need more self-care, and denial of our needs at those points is tantamount to a breach in trust with oneself.

- Consider committing to care for yourself, especially in troubled times. Then watch your trust in yourself blossom.

With self-trust comes self-knowledge. The self-care that attends to emotional needs is just as critical as that which attends to physical needs. Indeed, as we have seen, maintaining a clear emotional field provides the link between our tangible and subtle experiences.

- Consider taking time to sit with your feelings, to notice and acknowledge them. Give them a place in your day and honor the wisdom they bring to the choices you make.

Relationships and Boundaries

The ability to self-organize as an individual informs the boundaries we set in our relationships with others. An individual who maintains good boundaries and responds respectfully toward others is more likely to manifest healthy relationships with family and companions, community, and finally with our global ecology. The state of our global ecology's well-being takes its full turn and enfolds meanings back through life on this planet, various cultures, communities, and families and into the spectrum of dimensions of individual experience. We might say that our spiritual dimension—the largest of our inner world—is exactly the same terrain as the largest dimension of our outer world—universal oneness—although from a different perspective. When we are in good relation with ourselves, we are inherently positioned to be in good relations with all else. And when we are in good relations with all, we are in good relations with ourselves.

Every transaction is globally relevant. What we do and say has ramifications that ripple through our own being as well as impact others. For example, an individual we encounter can be viewed as the first stage of impact from our words and deeds. That transaction begins the enfolding of meaning through the subtle dimensions of all direct participants. For us, it might be a series of reflections—did I really say that? Oh my gosh, I see hurt in their eyes and I didn't mean harm. Where did that come from in my being? For those we encounter, the ripple similarly goes through various dimensions. We might say that what unfolds in us extends to enfold in others, and what unfolds in others extends to enfold in us.

- Notice the responses of those around you to what you say and do. Just as importantly, notice the meanings that ripple back through your being when you act or speak. Do you feel good about what you have done or said? Do you notice any questions within yourself about whether what you did was useful or not, respectful or not, loving or not?

In any transaction, for example in a workplace, a communication may go from an individual through a figure of authority to the next larger social arena. The individual's experience is thus communicated to wider and wider networks, stopping only when the meaning of the communication fails to resonate with an audience.

- Consider choosing to live with integrity so that your communications, as they are shared in wider circles, can inform others about you and your concerns in the most clear, thorough, and accurate manner. If this can be done in a way that allows, establishes, and fosters good relations with all others, then that is good. However, we need to recognize that sometimes pain requires raised voices to alert others to our distress, and this may make others uncomfortable.
- I invite you to speak in whatever way is required for your needs to be heard and acknowledged. Speaking your truth in whatever kind of voice you need to speak might make others uncomfortable, but if it is your truth, then it is your choice. Your voice, your unique perspectives and knowledge, are needed to make the world a better place.

The creation of satisfying relations with others is based on self-knowledge and boundaries and with an intention to allow others their own self-agency, autonomy, and boundaries. We've seen how detrimental it can be when we overreach or make assumptions. We've seen that it is up to us to promote clear communications that keep us honest and right with ourselves and others.

- Here is an opportunity to think about how and how much you organize yourself as opposed to how much you rely on others to tell you what to do. Conversely, think about how much you rely on others doing what you want them to do. Set boundaries on what directives you will accept from others and from whom you will accept directives on your behavior and speech. Set boundaries also on suggesting or demanding what others should think or do. Maintain boundaries that uphold respect.
- I invite you to sit with any feelings of discomfort that arise in your transactions with others in order to investigate the nature of the boundary breach that feels wrong, and then to respond in a way that rights the situation.

There is always a question of how much one must conform in order to experience a sense of belonging in a community. People who have had less depth and breadth in their experiences will tend to conform, and people who have a greater depth and breadth of experience will tend toward individualism.[1] But as we learned earlier, individualism carries a potential for selfishness unless it is accompanied by attention to the qualities that support life. Similarly, if these qualities are not adequately attended, conformity can overshadow one's potential to develop one's own capacity and make a unique contribution. Categorizing our experiences as either one or the other carries a limiting tone, but attending the qualities that support life provides a common denominator that allows the integration of conformity with individuality.

Several consideration come to mind.

- Think about where your priorities lie—with conformity or individuality—and consider the challenge of balancing the two.
- Reflect on which ways of being and doing you have adopted from your community. For each behavior that comes to mind, consider whether it supports any of the four qualities discussed here. Does it negate your ability to self-organize or does it enhance your self-agency? Does it promote your personal growth and understanding of the world? Does it create stress in you, or does it relieve you of your burdens? Beyond feeling that you are similar to others in your group, what meaning is carried by what you are doing?
- Think about your need to speak or act in a way that is different from those around you. Reflect upon what your words or actions mean to you and what they might mean to others. Does your unique expression support the process of cognition in others? Does it allow and encourage their self-agency as well as your own? Are you creating stress in others or yourself? If so, is your rationale for doing so rooted in the qualities that support life?

Relationships with figures of authority are particularly important because they provide the link to more resources and participation in the wider social arenas. These links make it possible for an individual to inform community patterns and processes, thus developing community capacity to meet bigger and previously unaddressed challenges.

- Consider approaching a figure of authority who most closely aligns with your point of view and strike up a conversation with that person.

Our health-care relationships are of course critical to our ability to maintain a sense of well-being in the face of distress, disability, and disease.

- Consider initiating a practice of self-care that includes attention to nutrition, exercise, and rest, because doing so will certainly help. Equally importantly, in doing this we will be better able to identify our needs in the most precise terms, and this will position us for a partnership if not leadership in our health-care relationships.

- When you feel ready, consider using health-care practitioners as consultants who have knowledge and resources you can tap— arrive at the clinic with thoughtful questions and an intention to take charge by sharing what will and will not work within your pattern of organization. Be prepared to walk away feeling a sense of ownership, satisfaction, and hope.

Relationships are the substance of the networks that hold us all together and keep us alive. When a single person is not clear in their communications, whether intentional or unintentional, the effects of that misrepresentation of who that person is doesn't just affect that single transaction. It sets up dissonance throughout all inner dimensions of the speaker, making self-knowledge all the more difficult. As difficult as this is, it is important to acknowledge when we've said or done something that seems out of character. The dissonance provides the cybernetic feedback loop that allows us to correct ourselves.

- Think about what you know and what you don't know. See if you can find the precise edge between the two, and notice how your communications shift as you become more aware of what you do and do not know. Once you are clear about what you do not know, set yourself to the task of learning.

Sitting in a position of socially constructed authority creates dissonance within oneself and in how the role of authority is played out. It also creates a situation of distrust within the community. If capacity is not developed immediately, then those in our care will be harmed. In order to regain trust, we must be clear about our capacity, and where our lack of clarity or understanding has hurt others, we must apologize to rectify the situation. Taking these steps will ensure ongoing clarification of communications at the community level as well as a degree of resonance that will foster cooperation and collaboration among individuals and groups.

- Consider committing to being as clear and honest as you can in every transaction, and when you find you have not been clear, do what you can to bring more clarity and do it with humility and apologies where needed. Do this not just for yourself, for your self-knowledge, your personal well-being, and your satisfaction with your relations, but also for the benefit of those with whom you are connected so they can also function as efficiently as possible.

Our contributions to the communities to which we belong are optimally an expression of our authentic identity and capacity. However, many communities are not yet clear about their history. Obviously, where records have not been kept or are destroyed, and where genocide has occurred, community identity is difficult.

- For those whose community identities have been maligned or destroyed, gathering what history is possible and supplementing that with a focus on the four qualities that support life would at least allow new identities to be established. This situation makes it all the more important to follow patterns of interest and creative impulses as these may very well inform us of our ancestral history.
- For White people, consider investigating your own family tree to see how your ancestors relations with others were constructed (by choice or by force). Consider looking at how your own relations with people from other ethnic groups has been informed by your genetic and family cultures.

Process of Cognition

The process of cognition is the quality of an ever-expanding base of knowledge and capacity, including self-knowledge and knowledge about the world. There are many dimensions we might explore over a lifetime, beginning with the sensorimotor world of an infant and expanding into social, emotional, concrete and complex thinking, psyche, values and ideals, and spiritual dimensions. Each new dimension emerges with new perspectives and solutions to the problems in previously substantiated dimensions. In this way dissonance can be absolved.

- I encourage you to honestly assess your dimensional capacity in order to become more conscious of where your development has carried you so far, and consider which inner dimension might be your leading learning edge.

New perspectives prepare us to contribute to wider networks as well as resolving previously unsolvable problems. Models of being and doing bestowed on us by our first primary caregivers are key to our later ability to add new perspectives. In his presentation about the "Psychobiology of Attachment" based on decades of research at the Harlow monkey laboratory, Gary Kraemer argued that our view of how the world should be is exactly how we saw it played out by our earliest primary role models. Those individuals and later role models continue to inform how we reach for sustainable patterns and processes and how we meet the challenges that come our way.

- Think about whether your first role models embodied the four qualities that support life. If they did not, consider seeking new and current role models who do embody these four qualities. If any of the four qualities is more difficult for you, find a role model who seems to easily embody that quality. A person with whom you can talk is helpful, but role models can also be found in stories in print or in films. Spend as much time as you want with that role model. Naturally, for live visits, the availability of your role model must be respected. In story form, a role model's availability needs only be restricted by your preferences.

As wider networks bring us face-to-face with different ways of being and doing, those who make it a point to learn from these differences will add to their own growth as well as improve their possibility for good relations.

- Consider seeking new perspectives as you participate in the outer world, particularly as you engage with people whose networks and ways of life are different from your own. If, for example, you are primarily a concrete thinker, consider adding more reflective time to your routine, or learn about a different culture via travelling in real time, in your reading, or in the films you watch. If you already use complex thinking to think about how different perspectives might work together or by including time for reflection on a regular basis, consider exploring your dreams. Each and every dimension offers something unique and valuable. Consider what you have previously developed and what might be added to your perspectives to enhance your experience and capacity.

It is impossible to say how much we are influenced by the dimensions we have not yet developed. Even if we haven't explored our dreamtime or creative abilities, or had a need or inclination to delve into past traumas, we can pay attention to our values and ideals by thinking about what is important to us and how that drives our relations with others.

- Consider reflecting on what values drive your interests and relationships. Notice patterns that make you uncomfortable, and rather than judging yourself or others, consider whether a focus on different values might lead to a more satisfying experience.

Learning can be hard because some material and ideas are difficult to incorporate into our way of thinking. Sometimes new ideas in the form of other people's ways of being and doing appear just plain wrong because they don't fit with our ideas about how the world should be. However, when we use expressive writing to confront new material or ideas as we are confronted by what is new, in the way that Pennebaker and Smyth explain in their *Opening Up* volume, we can move forward more efficiently.

- Consider confronting, in writing or speech, something uncomfortable or confusing. Bring your full self, including your thoughts and emotions, to the task to explore who you are in relation with the new as well as what the new is in relation to who you are.

Dissipative Structure

The dissipative structure is comprised of the components of our patterns and their connections with one another. It allows us to flip the entropic spiral when things go wrong, and instead of moving into our demise, we can begin to flourish in the middle of chaos.

- Look for opportunity in the mess, to take from it what is useful and to discard what is not. When you are overwhelmed by the melee, consider creating a path that links your thoughts and feelings through writing or some other creative activity. If there is no time that can be set aside, commit to simply following your breath while you wash the dishes.

Our experiences are the components of our being that must be linked in order for us to stay alive and well. We have seen that connections among the dimensions of our experience occur as we occupy ourselves with what matters. We have also seen that development of the more complex dimensions can bring new perspectives that enable us to reorganize ourselves into more satisfactory patterns of being and doing when our old patterns are no longer useful. Even, and perhaps especially, in uncomfortable or harmful situations the information these subtle dimensions provide can bring balance and insight.

- Notice in which dimension you experience the most distress and explore what you know about your more complex and subtle dimensions in search of a perspective that can provide insight about what has caused you distress.

If your distress is primarily focused in the social and emotional dimensions, eliciting participation from any of the more subtle dimensions might alter your experience either through raising your vibratory pattern or by literally changing your interpretation of your experience.

- Consider each subtle dimension for its perspective on your distress until you find a perspective that gives clarity about who you are, what you need, and where your boundaries lie. Once clear, if your distress is not easily resolved, consider exploring the outer world for solutions. Seek help from those in power to build the boundaries you need because others will need this also. Seek help to change the power structures that interfere with our respectful treatment of one another.

Participation among our many dimensions conjures up an experience of internal support and feelings of self-sufficiency. Even when we need to reach for external support we can support ourselves from the inside also, engaging in a form of internal self-care while we deal with the outer world. Our more subtle and expansive dimensions can cradle those that are more tangible, providing us with the space and time needed for us to reorganize ourselves.

- Find ways to cradle yourself from within when you are unhappy or in pain.

Meaning

Meaning is what informs and energizes participation. It can be described as what informs every manifestation and simultaneously as the interpretation of significance for every event. In our human experience, we simultaneously interpret each event according to the various dimensional languages where resonance occurs. In every case, the resonance signals either support for or challenge to our well-being. Events that are significant to our physical body either support our bodily health or challenge it. Similarly, each other dimension registers the significance of every event as either supportive or challenging. If the event is not relevant to some dimension, it will not register as either supportive or challenging. We literally die when we no longer find resonance in our experiences,[2] so even meanings that are challenging or uncomfortable are, in a way, good. They inform us of what needs to change. Without that discomfort, we cannot know there is a problem.

- Consider sitting with your discomfort long enough to discover something about it and yourself. See if there is a new perspective or metaphorical value to be gained before taking action to make yourself feel better. Once you are ready to move forward, follow Frankl's sage advice and do something meaningful.[3]

If Capra and Luisi are correct that meaning helps us make sense of our inner and outer worlds, then meaning can help us make sense of chronic illness and other distressing situations. Some of Charmaz's chronically ill research subjects lived satisfying, if not longer lives because they were able to find new meaning, and in that, a more coherent view of themselves and their situations.[4] Making sense of things is the basis for how we organize ourselves, and this supports our self-agency, autonomy, and ability to adapt by generating a new self-organizing pattern that includes complicating factors.

For victims of social injustice (feeling miffed does not count), any adaptation can mean the difference between life or death, and neither outcome is ever certain. Options for creating a self-organizing pattern may be severely limited in terms of basic survival choices of diet, sleep-wake patterns, type of employment, and living conditions. Oppression, no matter how subtle, is life threatening.

- For readers who feel trapped between staying alive in an oppressive situation and reaching for self-agency that would more readily create a feeling of being alive, I encourage you to reach for a broader perspective and new knowledge, and to use to whatever choices you do have to support the presence of these four qualities in your life. (I'm sure many people who are oppressed do this already.) What may seem like small choices can add up to manifest a different kind of experience and can lead to the possibility of doing bigger things that are important to your survival and your ability to flourish. If nothing else, reclaiming some degree of self-agency begins to set a different tone in your relationship with your oppressive context.

I think that when we are in pain we become more conscious of the impact that meaning has in and on our lives. Symptoms cut people off from others either because they limit our ability to participate due to reduced endurance or because they demand we attend to our bodies in the moment. The fear of infecting others also limits participation. Whatever the cause for disruption of the network, the meaning of disrupted relationships enfolds back through emotional and mental dimensions and can wreak havoc with ideals and values of community life and spiritual oneness. The shifts in habits and routines and the loss of community for many as a result of coronavirus pandemic conditions are an example of how this can play out across a community.

The discrepancy between ideals and values and the physical or social incapacity to participate can lead to a serious breach in an individual's pattern of organization. When this occurs, adaptations must be made: the connections must be reestablished lest the breach cause further damage to body, mind, and spirit.

- Consider, prior to or in the middle of illness or distress, shoring up relationships wherever possible. Find multiple ways to participate and to engage with others. More avenues of communication will provide a stronger network that is less likely to break down when breaches do occur. Develop multiple ways to participate that support shared meaning in multiple dimensions of experience.

The experiences we garner in our participation with the outer world feed our spirit no matter how mundane the experience. To some degree, our experiences can be constructed to nourish our subtle selves in ways that will support our growth and development of capacity. Every opportunity to nourish ourselves with what we need is important.

- Choose your communities and your activities with your own well-being in mind. Consider whose influence you want in your life and what kinds of exposure will stretch your capacity to be the kind of person you want to be. Be self-organizing in how you develop your potential by adhering to what is meaningful to you.

Because meaning informs our tangible experience, we are called upon to search our inner selves when things don't go well in our efforts to participate. As detailed by Robert Ornstein and David Sobel in their first publication of *Healing and the Brain*, more than three decades ago, there is plenty of substantial evidence that our state of mind and social affairs impact our health. Many researchers in the interim have studied the relationship between mind and body, and between emotions and health. Pennebaker and Smyth note that the idea of pinpointing a specific psychological cause for a physical problem may not be easy due to a tendency to limit factors to a specific time frame or denial of what is uncomfortable, yet many researchers, including themselves, conclude that psychological stress is a factor in illness, and that every individual will manifest health or illness in their own way.[5] There is still much that we don't understand about this.

What we identify as disease is actually our immune system attempting to manage stress.[6] Looking through the lens of the qualities that support life it makes sense that when faced with a stress, our pattern of organization is disrupted while we find a way to incorporate a new experience. The loss of congruity would naturally result in a breach of internal communication and a diminished ability for maintenance and repairs. This could easily appear as symptoms begging a disease diagnosis, when in reality it may be simply an indication of a need for time and perspective.

It is interesting that even though many ideas about obtaining health are contradictory and do not yield a desired result,[7] many people continue to search for a meaning or metaphorical connection to make sense of their experiences and to seek ways to return to a sense of internal coherence. That Louise Hay's book of affirmations for addressing various ills has sold more than fifty million copies provides strong testimony to the idea that spiritual affirmations are useful in reclaiming a sense of well-being whether formal research data has captured that or not.

In terms of our understanding about what supports life and the feeling of being alive, such affirmations are as valid as making an appointment with a physician, and the two options are not mutually exclusive. Valerie Hunt's research led her to the conclusion that addressing illnesses at more subtle levels leads to longer lasting health whereas addressing only physical symptoms tends to result in repeating occurrences of illness.[8] My personal experience suggests that addressing illness or disease by looking at its meaning across multiple dimensions can be a useful strategy for managing chronic and complicated health issues. Models of energetic medicine such as homeopathy, flower essences, Reiki, and acupuncture address issues of subtle meaning as well as the more tangible manifestations of those.

- When you don't feel well, consider searching out the more subtle meanings of your experience even as you seek to understand what is happening in your physical experience. Is your heart broken? Are you confused about something? Are you distressed by social, emotional, or mental pressure? Consider addressing your disease by addressing the meaning inherent in your subtle experiences—either through affirmations, reflection, counseling, or action to address discrepancies in meaning, or through some kind of reputable energetic medicine, or both. This is not an invitation to abandon the benefits of orthodox medical care if that is needed but to attend to your experience with a holistic perspective.

Participation of various dimensions of experience with one another through shared meaning is the basis of our individual human pattern of organization. Shared meaning comes not in a vacuum but in the context and form of how we occupy ourselves. Pennebaker and Smyth have found that the occupation of expressive writing can generally be assumed to promote the well-being of those dealing with health issues or emotional pain. Although their focus is primarily on blending mental and emotional dimensions in expressive writing, they also discuss how the dream world and social and physical dimensions can be included. It is clear from their research that expression of emotion alone is not enough to effect a change, and that a writing process that demonstrates increasing evidence of cognitive participation is most promising.[9]

- Consider developing a habit of writing routinely in a way that links your thoughts and feelings. Do so especially when faced with a problem that seems unsolvable or when you cannot see a way forward. Write your thoughts and feelings about the situation until a door opens and you see a way through, even if it is just a tiny step you might take and feel good about.

Although writing is an excellent option, it is only one of many possibilities for eliciting participation from multiple dimensions. Any creative outlet can be used similarly because multiple dimensions are inherently enjoined in a creative process. However, movement by itself, in the form of dancing or exercise, for example, is not enough to facilitate change. In fact, it may feed into a mindless state that prohibits perception of self-knowledge cues. Movement must be combined with thinking in order to create the kind of participation among dimensions that can elicit an experience of energy or stimulate creative problem solving.[10]

In my own experience, thoughts can be joined with physical activity by setting an intention such as a determination to sort through a problem in one's mind while washing dishes, splitting firewood, or walking. The effect may be more explicit and pronounced when the physical activity has a theme relevant to the problem. For example, when I find myself lacking direction, I walk to the top of a mountain while reflecting on my situation. In my mind, the physical movement jostles my thoughts into new configurations and engages me fully with the meaning of moving forward. The panoramic view at the top opens me to new directions. By the time I return to my daily life, I usually have a good sense of how I can move ahead in what I want to do.

- When you are distressed, consider engaging in an activity that carries meaning in subtle as well as tangible dimensions.

Accessing metaphor is an easy way to include subtle meanings as we occupy ourselves with the mundane and repetitive tasks of daily life. Metaphors have potential to elicit meaning from many if not all dimensions of experience. They can help us to interpret our tangible experiences as well as dream material while we build connections between one experience and another. One person I know views cars in the dream world as symbolic of life, noting who is driving and how safe everyone feels, as well as the direction and speed of the movement in their interpretations of their dreams. These points are then applied to their current life with an eye on what resonates. That same person has also noted that major life shifts are often accompanied by a need for a new vehicle. It is helpful to this person to apply this larger lens when dealing with vehicle issues.

- Look for metaphor when unexpected events unfold, to see if finding meaning in this way helps you incorporate important experiences into your patterns of doing and being.

Habits we would like to dismantle probably carry meanings that have skirted our awareness. If these are truly bad for us, then what draws us in? What components of our pattern (what dimensions of our experience) need more support? The topic of addictions is too vast to cover here, but here is an idea.

- Consider how your unwanted habits separate you from connecting with yourself or others and whether they bridge or build barriers to your experience of wholeness. It may be useful to continue reflecting on this over time with the expectation that new insights will unfold, and that unfolding will bring forth new ways of manifesting an experience that is more satisfying.

Recalling that internal experiences can be disruptive to our self-organizing pattern, we must also realize that acknowledgement of archetypal and spiritual values—genuine heartfelt acknowledgement in which the meaning of the value is highly significant—can and will create a cascade of change in our way of being. Dreams, thoughts, emotions, and social activity can now be influenced in a way that alters our understanding of those dimensions of our lives and experience.

This is not always pleasant. For example, when some come to this deeper realization of a need for community among different racial groups and recognize that their ways of being and doing have caused undue separation and have harmed others, their way of organizing themselves will be disjointed until every dimension comes into line with that newly recognized value and awareness. Thought processes must change to include the new realization, all kinds of emotions must be processed, and new ways of interacting with people of European descent as well as Black, Indigenous, and other people of color must be navigated.

- I invite readers to be brave when new realizations begin to bud. Let yourself be in that new awareness. Invite it in and trust that you can, step by step, do the work of developing new ways of being and doing that are truly aligned with your spiritual values.

We all experience an ongoing rise and fall of energy. Some of these waves are predictable. When required tasks hold little meaning, our energy for completing those tasks typically plummets. When presented with tasks that are more interesting, our experience of energy rises quickly to the occasion. But sometimes there is a mix that may be hard to understand. In my mind, this may be because we experience resonance in some dimensions and a lack of resonance in others.

- If you experience an unexpected drop in your energy as you proceed with a task, you might think about each dimension of your experience as it relates to that task. Figure 6.1 provides prompts for discovering the meaning in your task for each dimension. Use them in your reflections to write something about the meaning of your task as it applies to that dimension. If there are dimensions where the meaning is unclear or absent, that in itself is instructive. Notice also where the meaning in one dimension is contrary to the meaning in another. When this happens, look for a point of commonality between them and use that as a guide to move ahead. When any issues have been resolved in your mind and you can see a continual flow of resonance from subtle to tangible, proceed with your project!

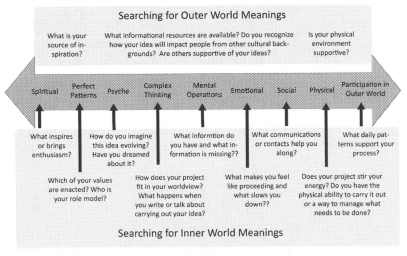

Figure 6.1. Discovering Shared Meanings across Dimensions.

It is clear that occupying ourselves with what matters is key to the possibility of a flourishing life, because what matters is life itself! How we engage in every activity and every role has potential to either support or undermine our ability to flourish. Although many of the roles we play are assigned by our various communities, we always have a choice about *how* we will participate. By this I mean that we can choose whether or not we will play our roles in a way that nourishes the qualities that will sustain our lives and the lives of others.

In a child's play, different roles are assumed on a temporary basis. In one sense this kind of play is inconsequential, yet in the course of the play itself, it is highly significant. In the longer term, the roles we assume in our play support what we do throughout our lives. Interestingly, all four qualities that are required for life are operative in play. If they are not, the fun ceases to be fun, play ceases to be play, the game is over and the players go home. Play is commonly understood to be internally driven (the self-organizing pattern). It provides practice in skill or role development (the process of cognition). It is creative and pleasurable (strengthening channels of meaning among many dimensions and thus supporting the dissipative structure). Play also informs and energizes (because it holds some kind of meaning for the players).

- Consider occupying yourself in a truly playful way—keep the game going by playing in a way that draws in companions or until any stress you are experiencing is dispelled.

For play to be creative, there must be a suspension of judgment. This is what allows new ideas to be considered. Conversely, narratives about right and wrong carry the meaning that perfection is a top priority. This is inhibitory because it induces an element of fear.

I do not mean to say that there are not better and worse choices. This entire book is dedicated to shedding light on what those better and worse choices might be. But along with those illuminations is a theme of ongoing navigation. This means doing the best we can with what we have, forgiving ourselves when we see that we have caused harm, and acknowledging what could have been done differently, and affirming an intention to do differently in the future.

- Notice your judgment when you feel stymied and stop to consider your next steps with a critical eye on the four qualities that sustain life. Develop habits that support these qualities in yourself and others. Pay attention to how you keep them present in your ways of living your life to the fullest extent possible.

NOTES

Chapter 1 Self Organizing Pattern

1. Capra and Luisi, *Systems View,* 305.
2. Wiener, *Human Use,* 28-33; Capra & Luisi, *Systems View,* 309.
3. Capra and Luisi, *Systems View,* 129; Maturana and Varela, *Autopoiesis,* 9-12.
4. Hasselkus, *Meaning,* 71-73.
5. Ibid, 73-74.
6. Wiener, *Human Use,* 28-38
7. Ibid, 95-96.
8. Hasselkus, *Meaning,* 72-73.
9. Hamad, *White Tears,* 50-52.
10. Hasselkus, *Meaning,* 25.
11. Hamad, *White Tears,* 50-52.

Chapter 2 Relationships and Boundaries

1. *Wilcock and Hocking, Occupational Perspective, 148.*
2. *Katz, Indigenous Healing, 295-310.*
3. *Hasselkus, Meaning, 107.*
4. *Schaef, Co-Dependence, 52-64.*
5. *Pennebaker & Smyth, Opening Up, 69.*
6. *Hasselkus, Meaning, 63-64.*
7. *Schaef, Co-Dependence, 52-55.*
8. *Schaef, Co-Dependence, 60-61; Schaef, When Society, 115-116.*
9. *Schaef, When Society, 106-108.*
10. *Schaef, Co-Dependence, 48-56.*
11. *Hamad, White Tears, 219.*

12. *Kendi, Stamped, 24-25.*
13. *Campbell and Moyers, Power of Myth, 4.*
14. *Hamad,* White Tears, *105-165; Kendi,* Stamped, *241-242.*
15. *Kendi, Stamped, 67-68, 83-84.*
16. *Hasselkus, Meaning, 29-30.*
17. *Ibid.*
18. *Schaef, Beyond Therapy, 191-193.*
19. *Katz, Indigenous Healing, 282-283.*
20. *Ibid, 283.*
21. *Ibid.*
22. *Schaef, Beyond Therapy, 194.*
23. *Ibid.*
24. *Kendi, How to Be an Anti-Racist, 106-121.*
25. Schaef, *Beyond Therapy,* 37-38.

Chapter 3 Process of Cognition

1. *Maturana and Varela, 1980, 11-12.*
2. *Ibid, xxi.*
3. *Piaget & Inhelder, Psychology of the Child; see also Piaget et al, Intelligence and Affectivity, 14 for a chart of developmental levels.*
4. *Maturana and Varela, Autopoiesis, 57-58.*
5. *Manser, Pages of Shustah, 98-104.*
6. *Ibid, 430-436.*
7. *Ibid.*
8. *Ibid.*
9. *Piaget & Inhelder, Psychology of the Child, 4-12.*
10. *Sri Aurobindo, Synthesis, 5-25, 12.*
11. *Manser, Pages of Shustah, 60-72, 98-103, 394-399.*
12. *Grof, Beyond the Brain, 36-51, 92-137.*

13. *Piaget and Inhelder,* Psychology of the Child; *Piaget et al, Intelligence and Affectivity, 14.*

14. *Grof, Beyond the Brain, 36-51.*

15. *Manser, Pages of Shustah, 98-103.*

16. *Ibid, 436.*

17. *Ibid.*

18. *Ibid, 430-436.*

19. *Grof, Beyond the Brain, 92-137.*

20. *Ibid, 36-51, 92-137.*

21. *Ibid, 37; 93-95.*

22. *Ibid.*

23. *Jung, Approaching the Unconscious, 93; Henderson, Ancient Myths, 118; von Franz, Process of Individuation, 168-176.*

24. *Grof, Beyond the Brain, 93-95.*

25. *Ibid, 96-98.*

26. *Jung, Approaching the Unconscious, 93.*

27. *Manser, Pages of Shustah, 417-421.*

28. *Aurobindo, Synthesis, 6.*

29. *Chopra, Ageless Body, 167-168.*

30. *Campbell and Moyers,* Power of Myth, *60-61.*

31. *Ibid, 61. See also Pearson, Awakening the Heroes, 277-279.*

32. *Pearson, Awakening the Heroes, 5-7.*

33. *Ibid, 7.*

34. *Pearson, Awakening the Heroes, 27-68, 235-256.*

35. *Ibid, 15-19.*

36. *Ibid, 14-20, 76-79, 88-90, 96-98, 101, 110-113, 115, 131-133, 145-146,154-157, 1698-169, 187-189, 205-207, 212, 216-217, 225-227.*

37. *Ibid, 235-256.*

38. *Grof, Beyond the Brain, 98-127.*

39. *Manser, Pages of Shustah, 430-436.*

40. *Pearson, Awakening the Heroes, 237.*

41. *Chopra, Ageless Body, 167.*

42. *Grof, Beyond the Brain, 127-131.*
43. *Manser, Pages of Shustah, 430-436.*
44. *Hasselkus, Meaning, 4.*
45. Ibid, 95-96.

Chapter 4 Dissipative Structure

1. *Prigogine and Stengers, Order Out of Chaos, 292ff.*
2. *Hasselkus, Meaning, 177.*
3. *Charmaz, The Body, Identity, and Self,. 675.*
4. *Ibid.*
5. *Frankl, Man's Search, 81-85*
6. *Hasselkus, Meaning, 96.*
7. *Capra, Uncommon Wisdom, 122*
8. *Schaef, Co-Dependency, 27*
9. *Bohm, Unfolding Meaning; Bohm, A New Theory; Bohm, Implicate Order; Peat, Infinite Potential, 258.*
10. *Bohm, A New Theory, 281*
11. *Ibid.*
12. *Ibid, 281.*
13. *Charmaz, The Body, Identity, and Self, 1995.*
14. *Hasselkus, Meaning, 64.*
15. Kendi, *How to be an Anti-Racist, 202.*

Chapter 5 Meaning

1. *Frankl, Man's Search, 82.*
2. *Capra & Luisi, Systems View, 308-309.*
3. *Frankl, Man's Search, 82.*
4. *Hasselkus, Meaning, 3.*

5. *Frankl, Man's Search, 17-100; Charmaz, The Body, Identity, and Self,* 658.

6. *Bohm, A New Theory,* 273-274.

7. *Bohm, A New Theory,* 278-283.

8. *Ibid, 275. Bohm, Unfolding Meaning,* 6.

9. *Bohm, A New Theory, 279-283; Bohm, Unfolding Meaning,* 15-18.

10. *Bohm, Unfolding Meaning, 24; Maturana & Varela, Autopoesis, xviii.*

11. *Bohm, A New Theory, 273, 279-280; Bohm, Unfolding Meaning,* 72-99.

12. *Bohm, Unfolding Meaning,* 90-91.

13. *Wiener, Cybernetics and Society,* 39.

14. *Bohm, A New Theory, 277-279; Bohm, Unfolding Meaning, 15-25; Wilcock and Hocking, Occupational Perspective,* 195-196.

15. *Wilcock and Hocking, Occupational Perspective,* 195-196.

16. *Bohm, Unfolding Meaning,* 90-91.

17. *Capra and Luisi, Systems View,* 303-306.

18. *Bohm, Unfolding Meaning, 72-99; Capra and Luisi, Systems View,* 303-306.

19. *Bohm, A Suggested Interpretation*

20. *Peat, Infinite Potential, 11-116, 221*

21. *Ibid,* 300.

22. *Capra and Luisi, Systems View, 304-307; Bohm, A New Theory,* 281-282.

23. *Hunt, Infinite Mind, 111, 292, 345.*

24. *Ibid, 28-29, 262-263.*

25. *Bohm, Unfolding Meaning, 1-71.*

26. *Hasselkus, Meaning, 4, 5, 6, 7, 9.*

27. *Ibid, 7-8.*

28. *Pentland and McColl, Another Perspective, 167-168.*

29. *Capra and Henderson, Qualitative Growth*

30. *Pearson, Awakening the Heroes, 14-20, 96-98, 131-133.*

Chapter 6 Decisions to Consider

1. *Hasselkus, Meaning, 4-5.*
2. *Frankl, Man's Search for Meaning, 81-91.*
3. *Ibid, 145-148.*
4. *Capra and Luisi, A System's View, 309; Charmaz, The Body, Identity, and Self, 673.*
5. *Pennebaker and Smyth, Opening Up, 7.*
6. *Ibid, 44-46*
7. *Ibid, 12.*
8. *Ibid, 136-140.*
9. *Hunt,* Infinite Mind, *232-275.*
10. *Pennebaker and Smyth, Opening Up.*

BIBLIOGRAPHY

Andrews, Ted. *Animal Speak: The Spiritual & Magical Powers of Creatures Great and Small*. St. Paul, MN: Llewellyn, 1993.

Aurobindo, Sri. *The Synthesis of Yoga* (6th ed.). Pondicherry: Ashram Publications Department, 1996.

Bohm, David. "A Suggested Interpretation of the Quantum Theory in Terms of 'Hidden' Variables. I." *Physical Review*, 85, 166–79. DOI:https://doi.org/10.1103/PhysRev.85.166, 1952.

_____. *Wholeness and the Implicate Order*. London: Routledge, 1980.

_____. *Unfolding Meaning: A Weekend of Dialogue with David Bohm*. London: Routledge, 1985.

_____. David Bohm. A new theory of the relationship of mind and matter, *Philosophical Psychology*, 3:2-3, 271-286, 1990. DOI: 10.1080/09515089008573004

Campbell, Joseph and Bill Moyers. *The Power of Myth*. New York: Anchor Books, 1991.

Capra, Fritjof. *Uncommon Wisdom*. New York: Simon & Schuster, 1988.

_____. *The Web of Life*: *A New Scientific Understanding of Living Systems*. New York: Anchor Books, 1997.

Capra, Fritjof and Hazel Henderson. Qualitative Growth. Accessed February 25, 2014. https://www.fritjofcapra.net/qualitative-growth.

Capra, Fritjof and Pier Luigi Luisi. 2014. *The Systems View of life: A Unifying Vision*. Cambridge: Cambridge University Press.

Charmaz, Kathy. 1995. "The Body, Identity, and Self: Adapting to Impairment." *The Sociological Quarterly*, 36, no. 4, 657–80, http://www.jstor.org/stable/4121346.

Chopra, Deepak. *Ageless Body, Timeless Mind: The Quantum Alternative to Growing Old*. New York: Harmony Books, 1993.

Frankl, Viktor. *Man's Search for Meaning.* New York: Simon & Schuster, 1984.

Grof, Stanislav. *Beyond the Brain: Birth, Death, and Transcendence in Psychotherapy.* New York: State University of New York Press, 2010.

Hamad, Ruby.. *White Tears/Brown Scars: How White Feminism Betrays Women of Color.* New York: Catapult, 2020.

Hasselkus, Betty Risteen. *The Meaning of Everyday Occupation.* West Deptford, NJ: Slack Publications, 2011.

Hay, Louise. *Heal Your Body: The Mental Causes for Physical Illness and the Metaphysical Way to Overcome Them.* Santa Monica, CA: Hay House, 2005.

Henderson, Joseph L. "Ancient Myths and Modern Man." In *Man and His Symbols,* edited by Carl G. Jung, 104-157. Garden City, NY: Doubleday, 1964.

Hunt, Valerie. *Infinite Mind: Science of the Human Vibrations of Consciousness.* Malibu, CA.: Malibu Publishing Co, 1996.

Jung, Carl G. "Approaching the Unconscious." In *Man and His Symbols,* edited by Carl G. Jung, 158-229. Garden City, NY: Doubleday, 1964.

Katz, Richard. *Indigenous Healing Psychology: Honoring the Wisdom of the First Peoples.* Rochester, VT: Healing Arts Press, 2017.

Kendi, Ibram. *Stamped from the Beginning: The Definitive History of Racist Ideas in America.* London: Vintage Digital, 2017.

————. *How to Be an Antiracist*, New York: One World, 2019.

Kraemer, Gary. "Psychobiology of Attachment." Paper presented at the American Occupational Therapy Annual Conference, Chicago, Illinois, 1996.

Manser, Ann. "Pages of Shustah." Unpublished manuscript. Loose-leaf edition available from the Temple of the Living God, St Petersburg, FL, 1974.

Maturana, Humbert and Francisco Varela. *Autopoiesis and Cognition: The Realization of the Living* (Boston Studies in the Philosophy of Science, Vol. 42). Part of: Boston Studies in the Philosophy and History of Science (207 Books). Boston, MA: D. Reidel Publishing Co, 1980.

Ornstein, Robert and David Sobel. *The Healing Brain: Breakthrough Medical Discoveries about How the Brain Keeps Us Healthy.* New York: Simon & Schuster, 1988.

Pearson, Carol. *Awakening the Heroes Within: Twelve Archetypes to Help Us Find Ourselves and Transform Our World.* New York: HarperCollins, 1991.

Peat, F. David. *Infinite Potential: The Life and Times of David Bohm.* Reading, MA: Addison Wesley, 1997.

Pennebaker, James and Joshua Smyth. *Opening up by Writing it Down: How Expressive Writing Improves Health and Eases Emotional Pain.* New York: Guilford Press, 2016.

Pentland, Wendy and Mary Ann McColl. "Another Perspective on Life Balance: Living in Integrity with Values." In Kathleen Matuska and Charles Christiansen's (Eds.) *Life Balance: Multidisciplinary Theories and Research.* Thorofare, NJ : SLACK Inc, 2009.

Piaget, Jean, TA Brown, CE Kaegi, and Mark Rosenzweig. *Intelligence and Affectivity: Their Relationship during Child Development.* Palo Alto, CA: Annual Reviews Inc, 1981.

Piaget, Jean and Barbel Inhelder. *The Psychology of the Child.* New York: Basic Books, 1969.

Prigogine, Ilya and Isabelle Stengers. *Order out of Chaos: Man's New Dialog with Nature.* New York: Bantam Books, 1984.

Rogers, Carl. "Empathic: An Unappreciated Way of Being." *The Counseling Psychologist,* 5, no. 2 (June 1): 2-10, 1975.

Sams, Jamie and David Carson. *Medicine Cards: The Discovery of Power through the Ways of Animals.* Sante Fe, NM: Bear & Co, 1988.

Schaef, Ann Wilson. *Co-Dependence: Misunderstood—Mistreated.* New York: HarperCollins, 1986.

_____. *When Society Becomes an Addict.* NY: Harper & Row, 1987.

_____. *Beyond Therapy, Beyond Science: A New Model for Healing the Whole Person.* Lincoln, NE: iuniverse.com, Inc, 2000.

von Franz, M. -L. "The Process of Individuation." In *Man and His Symbols,* edited by Carl G. Jung, 158-229. Garden City, NY: Doubleday, 1964.

Wiener, Norbert. *The Human Use of Human Beings: Cybernetics and Society.* Boston: Houghton Mifflin Company, 1954.

Wilcock, Ann and Clare Hocking. *An Occupational Perspective of Health* (3rd ed.). Thorofare, NJ: Slack Publications, 2015.

ABOUT THE AUTHOR

PATRICIA GAILEY, PH.D, has a background in occupational therapy and higher education. She brings more than 30 years of experience helping people navigate difficulties in home and community settings to her current roles as *Fundamentals* author, educator, and coach. She is active in Quaker communities and enjoys reading, film, making music, making things, and spending her time with family and friends among the trees and hills of Kentucky.

Printed in the United States
by Baker & Taylor Publisher Services